HOPE THOU IN GOD

By Vance Havner

BY THE STILL WATERS
THE SECRET OF CHRISTIAN JOY
ROAD TO REVIVAL
HEARTS AFIRE
DAY BY DAY
REPENT OR ELSE
TRUTH FOR EACH DAY
PEACE IN THE VALLEY
WHY NOT JUST BE CHRISTIANS?
PEPPER 'N SALT
JESUS ONLY
IN TIMES LIKE THESE
THREESCORE AND TEN
SONG AT TWILIGHT
THOUGH I WALK THROUGH THE VALLEY
ALL THE DAYS
HOPE THOU IN GOD

VANCE HAVNER

Fleming H. Revell Company
Old Tappan, New Jersey

Library of Congress Cataloging in Publication Data

Havner, Vance, 1901-
   Hope thou in God.

   1. Consolation. I. Title.
BV4909.H38 1978   242'.4   77-20228
ISBN 0-8007-0902-0

Contents

1	"Hope Thou in God"	9
2	The Felling of the Trees	11
3	"I Ain't Got Long to Stay Here"	13
4	Valleys	15
5	The Greening Willow	18
6	"There's Always Sumpin"	20
7	The Reminding Rooster	22
8	Thoughts While I Wait	25
9	Passport to Paradise	27
10	Forty Days	29
11	Just Heartbeats From Heaven!	32
12	"My Ways Are Not Your Ways"	34
13	For Saints Under Pressure	37
14	"Intending After Easter"	39
15	Something in the Side Pocket	41
16	"Fine, General!"	43
17	See You at the Homecoming!	46
18	Hear the Train Blow	48
19	The Christ of the Lonely Road	51
20	Make Mine Vanilla	53
21	Crossing Bridges Ahead of Time	55
22	The Buick Again . . . Postscript	57
23	God of the Valleys	60
24	"Out of" or "About"	62
25	God's Extras	64
26	"Backtracking"	66

27 A Charleston Snapshot   68
28 I'll Soon Find Out!   70
29 Home Before Dark   72
30 Go Home and Tell   75
31 From Myrtles to Blackpolls   77
32 The Puzzle-Picture   79
33 "Awake, Dear?"   81
34 Christmas Again   83
35 "The Patience of Unanswered Prayer"   85
36 Stroller in Snow   88
37 The Vanishing Pedestrian   90
38 Since You Went Away   92
39 Seekers of Signs   95
40 Touch Him and Tell It!   97
41 Last Run   99
42 The Mansion and the Mountains   101
43 Lifetime Semi-Retirement   103
44 "To Finish with the Scroll"   105
45 Songs in Winter   110
46 Along About Milking Time   112
47 The "Withness" of It   114
48 Look Who's Here!   116
49 The Underprivileged   119
50 Waiting   121
51 "No Night There"   124
52 Almost Time to Go   126

HOPE THOU IN GOD

1

"Hope Thou in God"

In the motel room I wearily set down my bags and prepared for a week's stay. I had left a sick wife in the hospital. I was following my doctor's advice to get away for a few days, after weeks of watching by her bedside. I knew it would be a difficult week, with myself in one place and my heart in another. I glanced at a table where a Gideon Bible lay opened. I do not attach undue significance to such things, but sometimes the Old Book has opened, as though by design, just to meet the need of that day.

It does not happen often that one finds the same verse three times on one page. It was Psalms 42:5 and 11 and 43:5. With slight variations the verses read: "Why art thou cast down, O my soul? and why art thou disquieted within [in] me? hope thou in God: for I shall yet praise him for the health [help] of his [my] countenance and my God." The psalmist was at a record low. His heart panted after God. His tears had been his meat day and night. His enemies taunted him, asking, "Where is your God?" He remembered the great days when he had been with the multitude in God's house praising and rejoicing, but look at him now! It is like Paul dropping from third heaven to his thorn in the flesh. (*See* 2 Corinthians 12:2.)

Have you ever known days when you remembered that great revival you had been in, where you had thought you could never again feel like this? Where is that joy and why is your soul cast down and disquieted? Well, thinking of David, Jeremiah, Paul in his low days, and John the Baptist in prison ought to help. And there was even a time when the Lord Himself said, "Now is my soul troubled; and what shall I say?" (John 12:27).

We are human beings making our way through a world as changeable as the weather with the very next hour unpredictable—shadow and sunlight, heartbreaks and hallelujahs, all mixed with no rhyme or reason as far as we can see. The day that breaks in glory may end in grief. The vacation trip that began in glee may end in a funeral parlor by night. It happens all the time. And even the choicest saints know the *why* of the cast down and disquieted soul perhaps more than some who never rejoice in the sanctuary.

One thing is certain, if the soul takes the psalmist's advice and hopes in God, *I shall yet praise Him*. For the moment we rebel and almost resent the suggestion. How can I ever praise God again after this? We grow bitter when some pitying soul who has never *been there* recites all the clichés and platitudes. But it works. I thought I could never be happy again making my lonely way bereft of my companion. I do not understand the why of it all. That waits for heaven. But faith does not wait for explanation to begin praising. Faith does not wait to understand. We have His word, and if it were not so, He would have told us. In the meantime what are we to do? Sob and sigh until we die? "Let not your heart be troubled . . ." (John 14:1). We have control over that, we can worry or not worry. It is a different kind of joy, sometimes mixed with tears, but once you get it you know what I mean. Meanwhile we may live through weeks and months when feelings fail and nerves go on a rampage; but we hope in God, anyhow, even when it seems almost hypocritical. It is not. It is faith at its best, and one day we will reach that *yet* when praise rings its joybells in the soul. Some days are not easy, and you may want to lay this down in disgust. But it works. "Hope thou in God . . . I shall yet praise Him."

The lowest ebb can be the turn of the tide! There is a Way ON when you've reached Wit's End!

2

The Felling of the Trees

I am sitting in front of a lovely Bible conference inn that commands a breathtaking view of distant mountains and the valleys between. That view is partly obstructed by tall trees that have grown up in profusion. Beautiful trees they are and there is always a pang of regret when they topple. Joyce Kilmer comes to mind with his lines:

> Poems are made by fools like me,
> But only God can make a tree.

One might feel like filing a protest this afternoon, but there is another side to this matter, as there is to many matters. My old home in the country where I grew up faces the same problem. A panorama along the distant horizon is partly blocked by trees, and we must part with either the trees or the view. We cannot keep both.

There are times in our lives when the long-range vista that God has for us is shut out by things close at hand. They may be good and precious things like these trees; indeed, sometimes infinitely more precious. Sometimes we must dispose of them, cut off the right hand or pluck out the eye, as our Lord put it, in favor of something better. Again, God may remove a tree so loaded with memories, so dear to the heart, that we rebel inwardly and languish in our grief. It may be a loved one cut down by death, and the soul cries "Why?" But if we are God's children, the removal works for good, although it may be a long time before that good becomes clear to our vision. Grief sometimes clears our eyes to see distances we never saw before. Tears are said actually to be the best eye medicine!

If the Divine Woodman has felled your choicest tree, it may be to reveal blessings hidden beyond. Some of the trees He displaced will be replaced by new ones; indeed, the same ones planted by the Lord in the world to come. Nothing is lost, no one is lost, in the economy of God. I will therefore bow in acceptance of the felling of my trees though inwardly I weep. It has happened before, and I rejoice now in what I would have missed in the new landscape, sights I would never have beheld. A new vista may be waiting for the fall of some trees. Some you must clear out, some God will take away.

"In the year that king Uzziah died I saw also the Lord . . ." (Isaiah 6:1). The loss of good King Uzziah was a major blow, a *minus* of staggering proportions. But it brought a greater *plus*—"I saw ALSO the Lord." God gives a better thing than what He takes away. Be not desolate at the felling of your trees. It is not loss but gain, both here and hereafter.

3

"I Ain't Got Long to Stay Here"

This title is a poignant line from the old spiritual, "Steal Away to Jesus." It is not just a lament of old age. Sometimes youth departs this world before the senior citizen. Graves are all sizes. And even if the life span stretches to one hundred years, it is soon cut off, and we fly away.

But as this scribe approaches seventy-five he is aware of the law of averages and what category he belongs to. He has been around a pretty good while, as we mortals mark time, and memory links him back to a day utterly strange and almost unbelievable to a modern teenager. Youngsters find it difficult to visualize me living at the turn of this century, for this hundred years has moved faster than a thousand used to go. Whether I like it or not, "I ain't got long to stay here."

I view with concern my shortening stay. I am human and this is the only world I have known. With all its dangers, toils, and snares this life has been good to me, leaving many treasured blessings in my bank account of memories. I discern by now a pattern that did not at times make sense to me and often seemed a medley of contradictions. I hesitate to leave a life I have grown used to living and the earth which has brought more joy than pain. I face an unknown realm with a thousand questions as yet unanswered. But I am not facing nothingness. My past life has been but an anteroom to eternity, and I move into a world as illimitably greater than this as this world is to a butterfly emerging from a chrysalis.

Either there is uncertainty and despair, or else, there is the word of Jesus Christ who came here to be The Answer and to prepare us for that world He is readying for us. I am anxious to find out what lies behind that curtain which is not lifted or parted but does grow thinner as dear ones go over there to live. Like a wild duck, feeling the first hints of autumn, prepares to move to sunnier climes, I must be going soon. All the mysteries ahead I leave with Jesus. He has told me enough; the crumbs make me impatient for the cake!

My dearest said, as she prepared to leave the hospital, "I'm going home tomorrow." That stay at home was short for soon she really went home to be with Christ which is far, *far* better. I am going home soon either when He comes or if I get away before. Things that so many get excited about down here thrill me but little. I don't have time to get excited about them. I'm just an exile and an alien in these parts.

"I ain't got long to stay here" and, for that matter, neither have you! Lighten your pack, my friend, for you can't take it with you anyway. Having food and raiment, be content and remember that according to the Good Book, godliness plus contentment equals prosperity. It can't be long, it may be soon, and when we get across, we shall wonder why we ever fussed so much about so little down here. This world is our passage, not our portion, as Matthew Henry said long ago. No use settling down for we can't stay anyway. And "we ain't got long . . . ."

4

Valleys

Joshua was defeated at Ai because of the sin of Achan, and it was in the Valley of Achor that Achan was dealt with and the sin of Israel put away. If there is sin in our lives or in the church, we must face the God of the Valley of Achor and remove the cause of the trouble. When we do that, the Valley of Achor becomes ". . . a place for the herds to lie down in. . ." (Isaiah 65:10) and a door of hope. (*See* Hosea 2:15.) It is the way to victory after defeat and the only path to peace. Too many defeated Joshuas who are on their faces today need to get up and face the real problem—Israel hath sinned. There is a time to pray in abject humility but prayer alone will not get us through. The road lies through the Valley of Achor!

There is the Valley of Dry Bones in Ezekiel's vision of Bones, Body, and Breath. (*See* Ezekiel 37:1–14.) A church may have the bones of sound doctrine and the body of a large membership and yet have no breath—"an embalmed body where art has preserved proportion and form amid nerves without action and veins without blood," as Daniel Webster said. It may be a Sardis with a name to be very much alive but dead in the eyes of our Lord, "so prosperous that it is out of breath and so organized that it is musclebound" (J. B. Phillips). A mortician can make a dead man look better than ever he looked when alive, and there are certain specialists in religious work today who can galvanize corpses into simulated activity that would deceive the very elect. As the old hymn says, "All is vain unless the Spirit of the Holy One comes down" and we must meet the God of the Valley of Dry Bones and wait on Him praying:

> Breathe on me, Breath of God,
> Fill me with life anew;
> That I may love what Thou dost love,
> And do what Thou wouldst do.

There was the Valley of Ditches where the Kings of Judah, Israel and Edom faced Moab in battle. There was no water to be had, but God's prophet Elisha said, " . . . Make this valley full of ditches and I will fill this country with water" (*see* 2 Kings 3:16, 17). It seemed foolish procedure when there was no water anywhere, but in times of great need, God may order us to do what seems utterly ridiculous: "Dig the ditches and I'll send the water." When we obey God in such an hour, when His commandments do not seem to make sense, the Valley of Ditches will become the Valley of Deliverance. He is the God of the Valley of Ditches!

There is the Valley of Baca (*see* Psalms 84:6), the Vale of Weeping, and when we must go through sorrow, bereavement, and trouble, let us leave a well of blessing so that others who come after us may assuage their thirst, refresh their spirits, and cool their parched lips. Fanny Crosby traveled the Valley of Baca for ninety years and left wells of refreshment in the countless hymns she wrote. Never a Sunday passes that we do not drink from those waters. Leave a well in the valley!

And of course there is the last valley, the Valley of the Shadow of Death. But it is only Death's *shadow,* and if we face the sunlight, the shadow will fall behind us!

Ira D. Sankey, the great gospel singer and Dwight L. Moody's helper, was blind in his last days. When a friend visited him, Mr. Sankey found his way to a little organ to play and sing, "There'll be no dark valley when Jesus comes." That will be the end of the Valleys. But the God of the Valleys will be there to welcome His children home.

5

The Greening Willow

Down by the creek, on my favorite walking trail, are two willow trees. I'm ecstatic this morning because after a terrible winter, the willows are turning green again, and that is one of springtime's earliest signs in these parts. The cardinal has already seemed to have a brighter note, and the yellowhammer rolls his call with fresh enthusiasm. I think the song sparrow has caught the spirit as March begins to bridge the gap. Spring is our shortest season because winter gives up with reluctance and summer arrives with a blast of heat entirely too early. But what there is of spring is worth waiting for. I have waited for a long string of springtimes, and it looks as though I might enjoy one more.

The earliest tiny flower daring to emerge from a cold earth and the first robin's song take on a mighty value to the tired winter sufferer. They speak of resurrection, revival, a better day. The life to come for the Christian has no wintry note in it. There will be no night. What a prospect for some of us who never welcome darkness! It is a land where nothing grows old so it must have an eternal springtime. Though winter comes now, springtime always makes it and speaks of an eternal state of bliss—now so transitory.

On Paul's sea trip toward Rome we read that in the

fearful storm the voyagers ". . . deemed that they drew near to some country" (Acts 27:27). A little later they cast four anchors and wished for the day. Some of us who have been around quite awhile are aware by now that we draw near to the next world. We have cast anchors and wish for the day. Springtime says something to us that no other season can. The weeping willow has always spoken of sorrow and drooping spirit. How wonderful that the weeping willow should be one of the very first trees to give hints of better days!

It won't be long until the finches chatter busily in the budding trees and the wood thrush begins his seasonal concert. The vireos and warblers will take over the tree tops, so full of *all of a sudden*. The myrtle warbler will head the procession, and I will try to make the most of the precious weeks until the blackpoll warbler brings up the rear.

Of course there is no perfect season in this poor sin-wrecked world. Even spring comes in with tornadoes and floods and there seems to be little order to the weather. But springtime reminds us of a better day, before Adam and Eve ate us out of house and home in Eden, and points us to Paradise regained in a redeemed earth. We welcome the faintest indications of what was God's original intention and His final purpose. Right now, we are in the middle of the book of His Purpose and we are looking both ways, back at what has been and ahead to what will be. There is still enough renewal and beauty in this old world to tell us that it has had better days and that it awaits a renovation one of these days. My willows perk up my languid spirits on the threshold of spring.

Make sure that you, through faith in Christ, are part of that new race of the sons of God, the called according to His purpose. He would conform you to the image of His Son and then, for you, all things would work together for good. For all of us, redemption draws nigh. We draw near to some country. Let us cast our anchors and wish for the day!

6

"There's Always Sumpin"

It was Amos—or maybe Andy—who used to say it. He meant that life is one thing after another, and if it isn't this it will be that. There will be decisions to make, troubles to face, bills to pay, ups and downs. There's always something, never a time when there's nothing. Jesus said, ". . . In the world ye shall have tribulation. . ." (John 16:33). The word means *pressure,* and when have we ever had so much of that! We have invented a thousand sophisticated gadgets to lessen the pressure, and now we live on the edge of a nervous breakdown all the time. There is no escape from the squeeze. "There's always sumpin."

But what did our Lord say next in this pressure passage! *"But* be of good cheer." Good cheer when I'm

beset with fears and fightings within and without! The
Greek word for pressure here is *thlipsis* and I'm *thlip-
sified,* pressurized from all directions. Yes, I am to be of
good cheer, for this pressure is from the world and my
Lord says, in the same verse, "I have overcome the
world." He had a rough time in this world. The world
order, even the religious establishment, was against
Him, and He died on a cross, the emblem of suffering
and shame. If it had ended there, we could only say the
world overcame *Him,* but three days later He came out
of the grave. He defeated death, the last enemy that shall
be destroyed. He began a new race—a new order—and
conquered what everybody thought had overcome Him.

But where do we come in? Was this one isolated victory which we must celebrate from afar, or can we get in
on it? "Whatsoever is born of God overcometh the world
. . ." (1 John 5:4). All who are born again can rise above
the pressures of this present world. They transform some
things and others they transcend.

John proceeds further, "Who is he that overcometh the
world?" (1 John 5:5). The answer is plain, "He that be-
lieveth that Jesus is the Son of God." He has just said, in
the fourth verse, ". . . this is the victory that overcometh
the world, even our faith." This is a double-barreled
faith, faith that starts out with heart trust in Jesus Christ
as God's Son and goes on day by day *faithing* Jesus
Christ for every situation as it arises—

> Simply trusting every day,
> Trusting through a stormy way,
> Even when my faith is small,
> Trusting Jesus, that is all.

The discipline is sometimes severe, and the orders seem tougher than a marine sergeant's. The battle is not won on the parade ground but out in the thick of the fight.

Furthermore, while "there's always sumpin," there's always *Someone*. And He is with us as He said. Sometimes we find it difficult to feel that Presence, and we seem to fight alone with only the stub of a sword. He Himself was forsaken in His darkest hour, and Paul said ". . . all men forsook me . . . . Notwithstanding the Lord stood with me . . ." (2 Timothy 4:16, 17). If you feel deserted in the darkest hour, remember Another who cried, "My God, my God, why hast Thou forsaken me?" (Matthew 27:46). But three days later He overcame death itself. The lowest ebb was the turn of the tide. Your Waterloo is behind you. He won the battle and you share in the power of His resurrection. If He did it, you can and will, for greater is He that is not only *with* you but *in* you than he that is in the world.

7

The Reminding Rooster

Just across the fence from the motel where I am staying this week in Florida is a small house, and whoever lives there keeps a most wide-awake and energetic little rooster. Long before daylight he is up and about. Sunup has never yet caught him asleep, and he announces the new day with a very loud voice for such a small rooster. When I wake up and hear him, I am confused for a moment. It has been a long time since I was awakened like this. Who expects to hear a rooster in the middle of a city in all this avalanche of tourists! (Each morning I watch the travelers pack up and take off, and when I see how much they have to load I decide that, although they may have come from Maine or Minnesota to get away from it all, it looks as though they brought it all with them!)

But back to my rooster. This morning he aroused tender memories of long ago on the little farm in Carolina. His vigorous reveille started a train of recollections rolling—the plain old house on the hill; the big oaks still standing; Father up before day to open his little grocery store long before the faintest possibility of a customer; Mother in the kitchen; the welcome smell of breakfast; and a little boy ready to start out with old Shep for a tramp in the woods. Life was serene and gentle. But now the little boy is an old preacher, nearing seventy-five, caught up with everybody else in the pandemonium that somehow is misnamed Progress. Thanks to you, young Chanticleer, for breaking into everything with a reminder that living has not always been like this and for stirring up a nostalgia for days beyond recall!

There was another rooster, the Bible rooster, whose crowing brought no such pleasant memories. It was the cockcrow that brought Simon Peter to his senses and the heartbreaking awareness that he had denied his Lord. The cock crowed and Peter remembered and wept bitterly. Not a few disciples today, like Peter, are warming at the wrong fire and need a reminder.

But pilgrims like myself need to hear, in all this modern bedlam, something to bring back simpler times and recapture, if but for a moment, what was once our regular experience. The little rooster this morning seems out of place in such a setting, but maybe it is we who are out of place, and we would do well to get back into his setting.

I notice that this little fellow is not at all intimidated or embarrassed amongst all the cars around, the planes overhead, and the stepped up pace of these times. He is just *doing his thing.* He has not modernized it or added new notes or made his performance contemporary. Some of us poor mortals would do well to just be ourselves and sing our song though some sophisticates might think it *corny.* Perhaps some weary travelers would awaken, as I have done these mornings, to reminders of a precious past or maybe to an awareness that we, like Peter, have denied our Lord. It will be good for us if we can hear above all the traffic the Reminding Rooster! After all, he is what he was put here to be and does what he was put here to do . . . and is not that what it is all about?

8

Thoughts While I Wait

If I had known, Dear Heart, how much I would miss you—although I tried to tell you many times how much you meant to me—and if I had known you'd go so soon where these eyes cannot see, I think I would have kept you in sight each passing day. How easy it is to assume that what is ours right now just can't leave us for many years ahead! And we never know how short is the priceless time that remains! We took for granted countless hours that sometimes seemed dull, but if they could now be bought, I'd give a year for just one of them.

To know not what we have until we don't have it; to never miss the water until the spring runs dry; to consider ordinary what should never be commonplace—that is the sad weakness we discover too late.

Many were the phone calls we made across the country and across thirty-three years. But now the communications are out; the operator does not answer; my credit card is no good for that realm; and God has closed all circuits for the moment. Our dear ones are with Jesus and Jesus is with us, but what that means in communication, I do not know. He can get to them and I can get to Him, but I do not know whether He relays anything from me to them. I know I am in touch with Him and that must suffice until all circuits are cleared and the lines are open.

The past three years of loneliness have made me a hungry student of all possible light on the state of our dear ones with the Lord. The Scriptures do not give us many details and countless questions wait for answers. God will not disappoint the countless millions who have cushioned their tired heads and dried their tearful eyes with the available facts, and the Father will see to it that reality will far exceed our fondest hopes. To be with Christ is *far, far* better and the word for that fact is *superlative*. It will be so much better than our poor imaginations can only surmise, for eye hath not seen nor ear heard nor can the heart comprehend what is prepared for us hereafter in this respect as in all others. Is it not enough to read that saints, then living, will be caught up *together* with those who have gone before, ever to be with the Lord? What more do you want? If there were no other word—and there is plenty more—this ought to send you singing through whatever time is left until He comes or you go!

While troubled or curious souls experiment with ESP, Ouija boards, fortune tellers, witches and all the rest of this pitiful questing, I have a Book and I have a Lord—a Lord who died and rose, who got in touch with at least three dead people while He was here and brought them back again. With a sample case like that, think what He must have in the storehouse of the Life To Come! It doth not yet appear . . . but we know that we shall be like Him and so will all the saints and relationships that were sweet and precious in this poor world. Think how all those buds will flower never to fade forever!

Yes, the communication is cut now for a season and I can't get through. The heart grows restless and the wait seems long, but we have all eternity to make up for it. We have not heard those voices, now stilled, for the last time nor have we seen those faces finally. What the new face and voice will be like remains to be seen and heard, but our present equipment would not be able to take it if we could. John had seen His Lord in the flesh for three years, but one glimpse of the glorified Lord knocked him out! It is only a little while until we are geared for that new age when faith gives way to sight. We can afford to wait. It will be worth it all when we see Jesus and all His saints in their new Easter outfits. Make sure you're in line to be fitted out like them on that Day!

9

Passport to Paradise

I am sometimes almost amused at the way we speak of *terminal illness* as though only people so afflicted were sure to die. You'd think the rest of us would live on here forever; whereas, a terminal case may last longer than we do! Come to think of it, every one of us has a terminal ailment: we are all going to die unless Jesus returns before our time. We live in bodies that are already deteriorating and will soon cease to function even if some accident doesn't kill us in the meantime.

If these lines fall under the eyes of some dear soul with not much more time left by medical calculations, it may help a bit to take a different look at this ailment that will soon terminate your earthly stay. If you are a Christian, has it ever occurred to you that however great your agony may be and how long the hours, this illness may be an angel in disguise for it is your passport to Paradise, the key that will ultimately open the door of the world to come. It is only through death that we change worlds. The agent of death turns out to be our liberator from this poor body to the new life, when the spirit goes to be with Christ, which is far, far better. Do not think then of your illness as brutally ending your existence but as a ticket to heaven. This is not to glorify death; for while we may glory in our infirmities, we are not to glorify them. Disease and death come as a result of sin but under God even they may work together for our good. You are not to be a victim of death. Death itself, the last enemy, shall be destroyed. But, as things are now set up, dying in the body only opens a new chapter that means ultimately a new body that no illness, terminal or otherwise, can ever touch. You can't lose for winning!

Our dying Saviour said to the repentant thief, ". . . Today shalt thou be with me in paradise" (Luke 23:43). As horrible as was the agony of the crucifixion, it was but the prelude to eternal happiness. "For our light affliction, which is but for a moment, worketh for us a far more exceeding and eternal weight of glory" (2 Corinthians 4:17). *Today* was an awful day for that thief at first but balance it over against *with me in paradise* and things take on a new perspective. In the most awful moments of his existence he was ticketed for heaven by the Son of God. If you are trusting my Lord, you are already cleared for Paradise, but death signs the last papers on this side and is forced to pay tribute to its conqueror!

"O death, where is thy sting? O grave, where is thy victory?" (1 Corinthians 15:55). Gone, if your life is hid with Christ in God! The enemy that took your dear one will, by the same procedure, unite you both again under far better conditions, if you are the Lord's. In your darkest moment, what seems a leap into the black unknown turns out to be portals to Paradise. It may seem an excruciating way to get there, but it will all be but for a moment. It will be worth a thousand deaths one minute after we reach that shore!

10

Forty Days

Throughout the Bible some very important things happened within periods of forty days. The Flood began with forty days and nights of rain (Genesis 7:12). Moses was on Mount Sinai forty days and nights (Exodus 24:18). When Israel rebelled, Moses fell down before the Lord forty days and nights (Deuteronomy 9:25).

Elijah went in the strength of angel food forty days and nights. (1 Kings 19:8). Ezekiel bore in symbolism the iniquity of Israel forty days (Ezekiel 4:6). Jonah declared that Nineveh would be overthrown in forty days (Jonah 3:4). Jesus fasted forty days and nights before His temptation (Matthew 4:2) and was in the wilderness forty days (Mark 1:13).

But most important of all was the forty-day period between His resurrection and His ascension when our Lord was seen by His disciples in His new body with infallible proofs that He had conquered death. We have heard it so long that familiarity with the account has dulled our senses, and what ought to make us shout for joy in church aisles, puts us to sleep in the pews.

Think of it, the Son of God fresh from the grave appearing here and there to a few followers for forty days! And here is a mystery of all mysteries that boggles the minds of us sophisticates nowadays. Why did He not appear before His enemies? What a dramatic scene, if He had stood again before Herod and Pilate! Why did He stay in an obscure Roman province with a whole world dying for salvation? Why not a showing in Rome, Athens, Alexandria? What sort of program is this, just letting the secret out to a few ordinary run-of-the-mill people? It is enough to give the news media a nervous breakdown! Wouldn't it have proven in days what we have tried for centuries to get across? The facts were all firsthand and visible. Those who crucified Him and those who witnessed Calvary were living, and He could easily have been identified. Today a preacher back from the grave would run every other news item off the front pages. And why not? Millions are dying, and we must get the word around. Think of what television could do with that! But had He chosen to show the whole world, our Lord would not have needed all our gadgets. Here were the most amazing forty days of all the centuries, on which all Christianity hangs and the Gospel depends. And when these witnesses started out to tell it, this was the heart of their message. He came back from the grave!

Somehow we have buried the story in all the pagan trappings of Easter, and we have had no small assist from the world, the flesh, and the devil. We have tried to capture it in art, music, and literature. You will search in vain our history books for much about it. Pages record trifling happenings that made no difference but, somehow, these forty days didn't make it. It is the way of the world and part of "the foolishness of God" whose ways are not our ways. God keeps a different calendar. With Him, in whose sight one day is as a thousand years and one year as a day, these forty days may have passed unnoticed in a world oblivious to what God was about. But to us who claim to know there had better be a reshuffling of our scale of values and a rediscovery of those few weeks that spelled the difference in everything for time and eternity.

11

Just Heartbeats from Heaven!

I have often wondered why Christians are not more excited about the blessed truth that we are always on the verge of eternity and that at any moment our Lord may come or we may go. I can understand why the non-Christian does not relish the thought. He is not ready for it and does not like to think about what it may mean for him. The worldling is drunk on his pleasures and abhors any thought of death or eternity. But why do so many who claim to be God's children take the prospect of heaven and eternal life as though it were a sort of fairy tale or coldly dismiss it as nothing to get happy about *now?* Some of them emphasize attending to our present business and letting the future be what it may. I know we are not to sit robed and waiting on some mountain top for the Lord to rescue us, but the just-be-faithful attitude betrays a lack somewhere. The New Testament saints were ready and faithful but they were also expectant.

It ought to mean more than it does to the professing Christian that he is a few breaths and heartbeats from the greatest experience possible to man—entering the new world beyond, discovering what things will be like when our bodies cease to function, and the other part of us, call it spirit or soul or personality or what you will, begins a new chapter. This is the only world we know and there ought to be at least a sense of adventure. What I will be like five minutes after I die is so stupendous a matter that it boggles the mind. The next world will not be geared the same as this one and we shall need new equipment. An astronaut getting rigged to go to the moon is but a faint suggestion of what will be necessary preparation for eternity.

The plainest Christian knows more about that five minutes after he dies than all the scholars in all the seminaries. Someone had that in mind when he wrote:

> Could I but win thee for one hour
> From off that starry shore,
> The hunger of my heart were stilled
> For death hath told thee more
> Than the melancholy world doth know,
> Things deeper than all lore.

How cheap and tawdry would appear the things that engross us so down here if heaven were taken out of the world of fancy and made an imminent certainty. What a shake-up of values and a regrouping of the important and unimportant! It would not mean idleness in pleasant contemplation. It would make us better workmen at our present job, shorten lonely hours, and smooth the bed of pain. It is easier to be a chrysalis if you are to be a butterfly!

Paul had a desire to depart and be with Christ. Heavenly homesickness is normal to a Christian, and I am surprised that I do not encounter more of it—not a morbid longing to get out of it all but to move up a grade. He is a poor clod who is content to stay in kindergarten forever. It doth not yet appear what we shall be but we have been told enough to brighten our eyes and quicken our step and to make even living in this vale of tears exciting business because it is an anteroom to heaven.

Some show more enthusiasm on the eve of a trip to Europe than saints soon to take off for heaven. We have ridiculed *pie in the sky* until one would think it a sin to sing "In the Sweet By and By." If we could recover our pilgrim character it might interest more earthly travelers in joining our happy throng. If tourism made trips abroad as dull as the saints think of the life to come, every hotel across the sea would go bankrupt.

Christians are always just a few heartbeats from heaven. It ought to make a difference!

12

"My Ways Are Not Your Ways"

When God began to reveal His plan of redemption, He started with a lowly peasant couple trudging to Bethlehem to pay taxes, a baby born in a stable and cradled in a manger, and that boy growing up to be the Saviour of the world, spending most of His thirty-three years on earth in a carpenter's shop! What was God up to? What if we had masterminded that Advent! Would we not have sent Him to Rome, Alexandria, and Athens? What a chance for press agents when the boy Jesus confounded the sages in the Temple! What the news media of today could have done blowing up that boy preacher into a world celebrity! It is enough to make all reporters weep!

When Jesus finally began His public ministry, it was a matter of walking around in Galilee with a few fishermen disciples. His brothers urged Him to go up to Jerusalem and get before the public, but He was thumbs down on that. When He healed people, He sometimes said, "Don't tell about it." When He rose from the dead, He missed the greatest opportunity of going before Pilate and the priests to show Himself. We've been trying to prove to this day that He rose, and that would have settled it once for all! He put on no show, just said "Mary" to a weeping woman, broke bread in the home of two grieving disciples, and, to other sad followers, He merely said, "Cast the net on the right side of the ship and you will catch fish." (*See* John 21:6.) What commonplace ways of breaking the greatest news ever made known to men!

God didn't do it our way. And somewhere hidden in all this is something we haven't caught onto yet. The devil tried to seduce our Lord into the show business by asking Him to jump off the temple. He failed but he has been more successful with us disciples. We have tried to make the Gospel a show, a circus, a theatrical extravaganza, making spectacular what began so simply, playing fortissimo what He started in low key. We are blasting ear drums in the name of Him whose voice never cried aloud in the streets. Somewhere we have misread our script!

We can afford to wait for the real fireworks. God is going to change the scenario one of these days. There will be a demonstration that will make all our histrionics look like a kindergarten operetta. There will be the sound of a trumpet and the voice of an archangel heard worldwide without radio. There will be angels and saints so innumerable as to boggle the mind, paralyze our mathematics, stop all our calculators, and confound all our computers. When the Lord walked on earth as a man, John laid his head on the Saviour's breast, but when John saw the glorified Christ on Patmos he fell like a dead man. Think of that day when the King of Kings and Lord of Lords shall appear and every eye shall see Him! Think of hearing the Hallelujah Chorus sung the way they sing it in heaven!

When the opera goers pass by in their dress suits and gowns headed for the Metropolitan, tell them: "You ain't heard nothin' yet! I'm waiting for the Big Event when God stages His Son's return to the earth that crucified Him, when all who are ready for the Great Getting-up Morning shall put on their Easter outfits and the saints go marching home with their troubles behind them, their questions all answered, and their tears all wiped away!"

13

For Saints Under Pressure

The child of God, "pressed by many a foe," may sometimes wonder why worldlings seem to be happier and untroubled by the plagues that beset him. He may ask, "Why do I read my Bible and pray and seek to be holy and yet am often cast down by doubts and fears while the children of this world seem less burdened than I?"

At such times we forget that the god of this age has blinded the minds of sinners and numbed them against those things that disturb the Christian. Satan's tranquilizers soothe the ungodly with a false peace and a superficial joy. The drugs we hear so much about nowadays are not the only sedatives. Satan produces mental and spiritual anesthetics more potent than any shot from a needle.

Let the Christian also remember that the man who seeks seriously to know and follow Christ makes himself thereby the target of the powers of darkness. Satan does not bother those who are already his but concentrates his fire on the children of light. A godly believer is a threat to the kingdom of evil. Most church members do not give the devil enough trouble to attract his attention! But if you are hard pressed by the foe, it means that you are headed upward and, having no fellowship with the un-fruitful works of darkness, you turn the light on them and show them up by contrast. This is very irritating to all who live in the dark.

Never forget that living the Christian life is a profoundly serious matter. Few there be who travel the Straight and Narrow Way, and all such walk in the fear of the Lord. The new version, with all the showmanship and glamour, the ecstasies and the foot-stomping of the Happiness Boys, finds no counterpart in the Scriptures with those who travel often the road of pain and loneliness in the fellowship of Christ's sufferings. Doctor R. A. Torrey said well that those who think they have reached some sublime height, because they never know any agony in faith and prayer, have gotten beyond their Lord and God's greatest heroes of the past. "In the world ye shall have tribulation" said our Lord. He said next, ". . . but be of good cheer" (John 16:33). The joy of the Lord, however, is not what the world calls happiness, which should be spelled *happen-ness* because it depends on what happens. It is the joy that could cry from prison, "Rejoice in the Lord alway: and again I say, Rejoice" (Philippians 4:4).

After all, our Lord walked this way first and He walks it with you. If you sometimes cannot read the signs and cannot see a visible way, remember what the African guide said to the bewildered traveler in the jungle, "There is no way . . . I AM THE WAY."

14

"Intending After Easter"

Luke tells us that Herod put Peter in prison "intending after Easter" (*see* Acts 12:4) to bring him forth publicly. Easter here means Passover but the phrase *intending after Easter* intrigues many Bible readers and has been a text for many discourses. *Easter* is a heathenish word, all tangled up as it is with Ishtar, the pagan goddess. We are stuck with the word as we are with so much of the trappings of the world in the worship of the church. The best we can do is to take advantage of the occasion to preach the Resurrection.

The Resurrection was a one-time event of all history. It is an annual on the church calendar. It is a weekly observance, for every Lord's Day is Resurrection Day. Every day is Resurrection Day for the Christian because he lives by the life of the risen Christ. The tragedy is that what should be an experience has become a performance. One feels like asking the Easter crowds at church: "What do you intend to do *after Easter?*" What difference will the Resurrection make in the way you live? How much does it matter to you that "up from the grave He arose?"

Well, how much difference *does* it make? Paul tells us

in the great Resurrection Chapter, the fifteenth of First Corinthians: *If Christ did not rise, our preaching is in vain.* It is an exercise in futility. Let the preachers turn to something else; they have nothing to tell us. *Our faith is also vain.* Christianity is based on superstition and hallucination. *We who preach it are false witnesses,* impostors, peddling a lie. *We are still sinners,* just as lost as ever, without exception, without excuse, and without escape. *The dead have perished.* We shall never see our loved ones again; they are gone forever. We have no hope for the future. *We are of all men most miserable,* death ends everything. What a difference the Resurrection makes! He *did* rise and we who believe are crucified, dead, and risen with Him.

How much difference should that make in us? *We should wake up:* "Awake to righteousness and sin not . . ." (verse 34). We are known by and affected by the company we keep. Paul warned the Corinthian Christians against the contamination of their vile and corrupt city. If we run with that crowd, we shall be infected with their disease. When did we ever need that warning as much as today!

We should walk in newness of life. That is the significance of baptism. Most church members show no evidence of a new life. They love what they always loved, go where they always went, do as they always did. If one is what he has always been, he is not a Christian, for a Christian is a new creature.

We should work. The great Resurrection Chapter closes with the admonition to abound in the work of the Lord. That means more than mere "church work." It means seven days a week. We are all in full-time Christian service, not part-time but full-time and overtime, for if we do only our duty we are unprofitable servants.

Wake, walk, work . . . that is how much difference the Resurrection ought to make. To do all three ought to be our *intention after Easter!*

15

Something in the Side Pocket

I carry my wallet in a side pocket. The wallet has never been too fat, but it has never been empty. There has always been enough to meet my expenses and something over. Our Lord asked His disciples, ". . . When I sent you without purse, and scrip, and shoes, lacked ye any thing? And they said, Nothing" (Luke 22:35). I did not set out long ago entirely without purse or scrip or shoes but I didn't have much. In 1940 I took to the road in poor health and with little money but with faith and a dear companion not afraid to risk an uncertain ministry. I had read the words of the psalmist: "I have been young, and now am old; yet have I not seen the righteous forsaken, nor his seed begging bread" (Psalms 37:25). I never owed but two hundred dollars in my life. I borrowed that from a farmer when I was going to school. My father always said that dirt, debt, and the devil were related so I made up my mind to keep as far from all three as possible. I had some narrow escapes in regard to all three but to this day have owed no man anything but love.

Everything is built on debt today, and the man who pays cash is viewed as a lingering leftover from another day. I have no organization, no secretary, no promotion gimmicks, not even brochures. In the midst of this highly geared world with the labyrinth of publicity machinery, I have run on a shoestring as they say. But there has been more than I need and always a little extra in the side pocket.

My God is able to make all grace abound so I, "always having all sufficiency in all things, may abound unto every good work" (2 Corinthians 9:8). Modern living is so complex and high-pressured that it seems almost terrifying to a country preacher who started when days were slower and more serene. I was never geared for the jet age and this double-quick pace. I have never learned the tricks of how to pull wires, politick, "know the right people," or get into the mass media. I just preach and write in low key on a meager budget, with no radio, television, or magazine. I never ran a school or a Bible conference. I am the despair of reporters and go-getters who look condescendingly on my little setup. But I've made it into my mid-seventies and there are more open doors than ever. And there's always something in the side pocket.

I'm all alone, no home, companion, or children. I could worry about what will happen in my last days. But He who has brought me thus far has promised even to carry me to hoary hairs. This present economy is working overtime with all sorts of programs for us old folks.

That is well as far as it goes and I welcome its provisions. But sometimes we get nervous and start looking to Washington instead of to heaven. There is nothing wrong with help from both directions, but it is blessed to know that we have a higher help when men fail.

There have been times when my finances ran to a scary low. I can understand the brother who said, "I've heard all my life that money talks, but all it ever says to me is 'good-bye.'" Many a time I have put my hand on my side pocket and thanked God that my wallet has never been empty.

There will be enough of all you need to do, all that God wants you to do as long as He wants you to do it. And there'll be something in the side pocket.

16

"Fine, General!"

Down in Florida, last winter, I met an old army general who had fought in World War II with George Patton in France. He related that one day during the battle of Normandy he was standing with the general when along came about thirty soldiers who were all shot up, most of whom would not live. He said Patton went over to them and asked, "How are you, boys?" Everyone who could salute did so and all said loudly, "Fine, General!" He related that, as he and Patton walked away, the great general was very quiet. "Finally," said my friend, "I looked at him out of the corner of my eye and saw the tears were coursing down his face." They called him Old Blood and Guts but that sight got to him.

I wondered if the present crop of boys would say, "Fine, General"? If the next war is atomic, we won't have time to find out! I wonder if we are growing Christians in that way. Long ago an old veteran wrote to a young recruit, "Thou therefore endure hardness, as a good soldier of Jesus Christ" (2 Timothy 2:3). He had been in many a battle and was all shot up; five times beaten with thirty-nine stripes; three times beaten with rods; once stoned; three times shipwrecked; a night and a day adrift in the deep; amid perils of robbers, of waters; by his own countrymen, by the heathen—perils of the city, of the wilderness; in watchings often, in hunger, in thirst, in fastings, in cold, and in nakedness. Now he sat, not in a cottage on the Riviera writing his memoirs but in a Roman jail awaiting execution, with stocks on his feet and bonds around his wrists. But if God had asked from heaven, "How are you doing, Paul?" he could have answered, "I have been faithful to the faith, to the fight and to the finish." (*See* 2 Timothy 4:7.)

The test of this business is not whether we are good on parade when the bands are playing, the bugles blowing, and the flags waving. The test is whether when the fighting is hottest, our comrades are killed around us, and we battle with the stub of a sword, shell-shocked, wounded, and deserted, we still can say, "Fine, General!"

> The strife will not be long;
> This day the noise of battle,
> The next, the victor's song.

We do have a General. A chaplain on Corregidor with Douglas MacArthur once complimented the general for faithful attendance at the services. The general said, "Chaplain, thank God you are not serving an ordinary four-star general of shortlived power and authority. You are serving that General described in the Book of Revelation who has seven stars, who is alive forevermore, and whose kingdom endures forever. Never forget that, Chaplain!"

We had better remember it! Our Waterloo is behind us, the victory is already won, and we are only engaged in mopping up exercises. But it is still a fight and sometimes we feel like we've had it. But

> Ne'er think the victory won,
> Nor lay thine armor down;
> The fight of faith will not be done
> Till thou obtain thy crown.

"Everything is fine, General!" It may not look like it, and we may not feel like it, but we are on the winning side. We may seem to lose our little skirmish but we can't lose the battle!

17

See You at the Homecoming!

Yesterday I visited a little town deep in the Carolina mountains. It was an annual festival where a multitude from the local area and many tourist visitors from without roamed all day through the booths and the entertainment area. They lined up for blocks for mounds of barbecued chicken with all the trimmings. The old country store was crowded all day, mountain music filled the air, and everybody was just having an old-fashioned good time. I saw no disorder such as scandalizes people about the rock festivals of this sick generation.

It was the nearest to a return to boyhood get-togethers of sixty years ago that I can recall. Of course the cars and clothes were different and the signs of modern "progress"(?) were there. But it did remind us of certain big days long ago—the Old Soldiers Reunion for instance, when the whole county turned out once a year at the county seat. The country folks were all in town, some by buggy or wagon, a few in primitive Fords, boys with their girl friends drinking pink lemonade and eating cotton candy. The old Civil War veterans sat around the courthouse telling about Gettysburg and Chancellorsville—their experiences from Manassas to Appomattox. I listened, pop-eyed, as they battled all over again.

Then there was the annual camp meeting each summer and homecoming day at the old home church. I plan to return there in a few weeks for the modern version of that great day. Almost all the old-timers are gone and I will be preaching to their grandchildren in the new church. There will still be dinner on the grounds.

There was something about yesterday in the mountains that spoke of a simpler day. It was about as near as we can get nowadays to what we used to be. It was more like real America, just folks having a good time together. (We should quit looking at television long enough to see each other and find out what we look like!) There was something homey, healthy, and wholesome about it, and it was at least a temporary antidote to the young generation burning out its batteries before twenty.

But it spoke to me of the future. God's old soldiers are gathering over there, and what a day it will be when all the heroes of faith, freed from all wounds and scars and dressed in their new Easter uniforms, recount their battles! And we shall be the eternal guests of the Great Captain who suffered most of all.

It will be *the great homecoming.* Our Saviour told us of many mansions in the Father's House and promised to return and escort us thither. One thinks of bygone reunions at Grandpa's and Grandma's when the family assembled for Thanksgiving or Christmas. How they went all out to have everything that would make it a great day for the children and grandchildren! Can anyone doubt that our Heavenly Father will spare nothing to make our

eternal homecoming full and complete when all His
children both in this world and in the next reassemble?
Jesus made it sound so homelike in John 14 that we find
it hard to wait.

See you at the Old Soldiers Reunion! See you at the
Great Homecoming!

18

Hear the Train Blow

Sometimes when I lie awake in the middle of the night
here in my apartment I hear the whistle of a little local
train shuttling back and forth among the warehouses de-
livering freight. Sometimes I hear our surviving pas-
senger train going through long before day. There is
something about a train whistle in the distance, late at
night when all is still, that awakens tender memories of
other days before the jet age clobbered us.

I used to ride trains all over America before I was
reduced to flying, which I do because I must. For many
years Sara and I spent countless days and nights on
Pullmans. There was something satisfying about board-
ing a warm sleeper late at night to ride along while sleet
beat at the windows. We loved the long trips to the West
Coast, watching sunrise on the desert, the mighty
majesty of the Rockies, and the relief when we reached
the California palms in our escape from winter. All of

that comes back with the whistle of a train, and memory visits the lonely hours. There is something weird and haunting that floats back across years never to be lived again, miles never to be covered, days beyond recall. It is akin to the nostalgia that strikes us when we hear a bit of true country music that reminds us of those early years when there floated up from the hollow below my old home the strains of "Red River Valley" or "Goin' Down the Road Feelin' Bad."

> Down in the valley,
> the valley so low
> Hang your head over,
> hear the wind blow.

I'm glad I grew up in the hills. Some of those fiddlers and banjo pickers from the hills might not have made it at modern auditions but their music was truly original.

So a train whistle late in the night carries me back to an age more livable. We didn't get to where we were going as fast as we do now but just what is there down here worth whizzing several hundred miles an hour to see?

And the train whistle reminds me that along with my train trips there has gone the dear one whose presence by my side made them such a pleasure. Trips hold little fascination now, for the biggest part of traveling was the sharing. I have not ridden a train since she went away, and although I keep thinking about having a try at what is still available, I think it might kindle a sadness that needs no extra fuel.

Well, somebody said, "Life is like a mountain rail-road" and I'm still aboard that train heading home. The jet age has made no change in that ride. The destination is the same and the fare is unchanged. The ticket to heaven was paid for long ago and no man pays his way. A lot of misguided souls think they are footing the bill but will wake up one day to discover that, as God said twice in His Book, "There is a way which seemeth right unto a man but the end thereof are the ways of death" (Proverbs 14:12; 16:25). The ticket was bought long ago with the blood of the cross and holders of all other passes will never make it.

Some who were dearest to our hearts have gone ahead of us on an earlier trip. I have been met by them many times down here. I am assured of safe arrival and a welcome no words can now describe. There are no wrecks on that line, and I am like the little girl aboard a train on a dangerous route in a fearful storm. When asked if she was scared she replied, "No, my Daddy is the engineer!"

So, when I hear the train whistle in the middle of the night, I remember that I am on a better Pullman than man ever built and I long to arrive in the morning.

19

The Christ of the Lonely Road

We have heard of "The Christ of the Indian Road," "The Christ of the American Road," "The Christ of Every Road." Somebody ought to write about "The Christ of the Lonely Road." After He fed the multitude He went into the mountain to pray and when evening came He was there alone. After He fed the multitude He sent the disciples away on a ship and was alone on the land. (*See* Matthew 14:22.) When they would make Him a King, He departed into a mountain Himself alone. (*See* John 6:15.) In Gethsemane He prayed alone while His disciples slept. (*See* Matthew 26:36–46.) On the cross He prayed, "My God, my God, why hast thou forsaken me?" (Matthew 27:46). He died in the darkness, He came out of the grave alone; He appeared to His followers alone; He ascended to the Father alone. He was the Christ of the Lonely Road.

God's men in the Scriptures were lonely men. Enoch's walk with God was a lonely walk because most of his generation traveled the other way. Moses spent lonely years in Midian and lonely hours on Sinai. Elijah stood alone on Carmel. Micaiah was an odd number as he stood before Ahab and Jehoshaphat and four hundred false prophets. Joseph Parker said, "The world always hates the four-hundred-and-first prophet." Jeremiah knew the pangs of loneliness and prayed, ". . . wilt thou be altogether unto me as a liar, and as waters that fail?" (Jeremiah 15:18). He was not a popular after dinner speaker! Daniel was an after dinner speaker on one occasion, but he had no complimentary ticket to the feast of Belshazzar nor was he drinking ginger ale with the potential alcoholics. They had to send for him when God wrote doomsday on Babylon's wall. John the Baptist with his leather suit and grasshopper salad was no favorite in the King's court and paid with his head for telling it like it was. He was not a guest in Herod's palace, he was a prisoner in Herod's jail. Paul sat alone in a Roman jail and said, "All men forsook me." (*See* 2 Timothy 4:16.) John on Patmos was a lonely saint on a dreary island in a restless sea.

The Christian is not a hermit, he must live in the world as it is, but he is often lonely in a crowd. He is a pilgrim but not a tramp, for he knows where he is going. God's prophet is a lonely man. When the storm comes, eagles rise above it but little birds hide in trees! And eagles do not fly in flocks!

Whether God's prophet or God's people, we travel a lonely road. The old straight and narrow way is not the thoroughfare of the multitude; few there be who travel it. We read that on one occasion every man went unto his own house and Jesus went unto the mount of Olives. (*See* John 7:53–8:1.) It is still like that today.

That Lonely Road is also the Only Road. No man comes to the Father but that way. There is a way that seems right unto a man but it ends in the ways of death.

The crowd is going the other way. Even the majority of church members follow the crowd. "Thou shalt not follow a multitude to do evil . . ." (Exodus 23:2). The Only Road is not crowded but the fellowship is good and there is a throng at the end of it, the host of God's redeemed whom no man can number. It will not be lonely forever. ". . . Where I am, ye may be also" (John 14:3). It pays to walk the Lonely Road if it is the Only Road. So let us bid farewell to the way of the world for only the way of the cross leads home.

20

Make Mine Vanilla

Ice cream in my boyhood days on the farm was a luxury far removed from the concoctions on today's fountain menus. If you wanted any, you made it yourself. That meant an afternoon of work. When the grinding was over, you had something that was cold, wet, and sweet but a far distant relative to the creations in scores of colors and flavors smothered in goo in today's ice cream parlors. By the time these exotic mixtures are rounded up with all the fruit, nuts, and syrup, topped with whipped cream and a cherry, you wonder whether you should eat it or just sit and admire it. Any bumpkin who would spoil the party by saying, "Make mine just plain vanilla," would be eligible for expulsion from the club.

Something like this has come over the field of religious experience. There are new fancy brands of Christianity never before heard on land or sea. Some are heavy with new theology and far over our heads. Some are charged with superfizz that leave us emotionally drunk. There are new recipes that make the church menu unintelligible to the ordinary soul. If your order doesn't call for a shot of some new flavor hitherto unknown you don't belong.

Recently I was discussing with a friend these late varieties of Christian experience and he, a quiet sort but with real character, said, "I've never had anything exciting or spectacular—just plain vanilla, I guess you'd say."

I've been on the road a long time and I have encountered all kinds. There was a time when glamorous testimonies of trips to third heaven swept me off my feet. Then I remembered that God toned down Paul's visit to Paradise with a thorn in the flesh to keep him from going around lecturing on his adventure out of this world and, instead, set him glorying in his infirmities and God's sufficient grace. Pentecost was a great day but the early Christians didn't form an exclusive Upper Room Club. Instead they *continued daily*. That is harder to do. It was low-key most of the time but it upset the Roman Empire.

By now I'm a little suspicious of the highly colored and richly flavored varieties at the religious ice cream counter. They are too rich for average blood and some servings make sick saints. Doctor James B. Gambrell wrote years ago about "the average Baptist" who "believes in simplicity, likes plain preaching and simple worship and prefers the plain, old level Jordan road, with a steady incline up all the way till it reaches the city of God." He opined that "if the choir by any machination of the devil falls under the lead of any professional musician and is turned to singing tunes with the delirium tremens, the average Baptist is grieved and solaces his soul by singing, 'How Firm a Foundation' or 'Amazing Grace.' "

Doctor Gambrell would find such average Baptists no longer the average and that goes for Methodists, Presbyterians, and all others. His comment will be dismissed with a smile and he will be disposed of by that great modern observation that explains everything: *times have changed.* But I find today even in young breasts a longing for some of that old brand of Christian experience and at that fountain I find myself saying to the Divine Dispenser, "Make mine plain vanilla."

21

Crossing Bridges Ahead of Time

"I'll cross that bridge when I come to it." We hear it often. The speaker means that he will not try to handle troubles in advance but will wait until he gets to them. Our Lord said, ". . . Sufficient unto the day is the evil thereof" (Matthew 6:34). That means every day has enough troubles of its own without borrowing from days ahead. Solomon and James warn us not to boast of our big plans for tomorrow since we do not know what the day will bring forth.

But I am thinking about this business of looking for trouble before it happens and dreading what we may never see. The classic example is found in the women going to the tomb of our Lord wondering who would roll away the stone. They arrived to find that an angel had already taken care of that! (*See* Mark 16:1–5.)

I must confess to a habit of wondering who would roll the stones away only to find that God's angel had preceded me and solved my problem. How often have I had to hang my head in shame for my too-little faith! But I am not the only poor soul who has moved in uneasiness about both past and future. You too, no doubt, belong to that clan that goes back to make sure you locked the door or lies awake at night doing mentally in advance what turns out to be a small matter when you actually reach it the next day.

I have accumulated a formidable list of disasters that never took place. Baggage that did not get lost, letters that did come although I was certain they wouldn't, ailments I was sure I had but no doctor could find. Job mourned that the thing he dreaded had come upon him. (*See* Job 3:25.) I could write a book about things I feared that never happened! Now alone without home or family of my own I find my situation fertile soil for growing all sorts of apprehensions. God has been so good to me, and I have felt so reproved when fears proved groundless and all things worked together for good. The angel had already rolled the stone away!

Then there is Mr. Fearing in *Pilgrim's Progress*. All

his life he was tortured by the fear that he might not get to heaven. But when the day came that he crossed the river, the water was lower than it had ever been before and he made it "not much above wet-shod." He might as well have enjoyed the journey all those years!

> When I tread the verge of Jordan,
> Bid my anxious fears subside.

But why wait until then? Fear not *now!* "I am with you all the days." (*See* Matthew 28:20.) So it reads in the Book and not "I will be with you some of the days." There may not be even a bridge to cross and your ghosts and hobgoblins won't show up. "Yea, though I walk through the valley of the shadow of death, I will fear no evil: for thou art with me; . . ." (Psalms 23:4). *Now!*

22

The Buick Again—Postscript

Readers of my book *Though I Walk Through the Valley* will remember the chapter "The Buick." In 1967, Sara and I purchased the first automobile we ever owned. I was sixty-six before I had ever bought a car—I wanted to think it over! Sara took driver training and studied her manual so much that I often said I wished I

knew my New Testament as well as she knew her Buick
book! We would start out with keen delight, she, driving,
and I by her side whistling, talking, or just looking. I was
supposed to pray while she drove but I often slept instead.

Then came 1973 and she went to be with the Lord, I
sold the Buick, for I had no thought of learning to drive
in today's mad traffic. I hoped that someone would buy it
and take care of it as well as Sara did. A lovely Florida
couple, who had heard me preach, came through North
Carolina on a vacation trip. They were looking for a used
car and bought it outright. It was a good buy. Few cars
are kept in such good condition. I could not bear to
watch it leave, for that Buick was tangled up in so many
memories.

Yesterday came the postscript. I came to Florida for
meetings and these two dear friends came to Jackson-
ville and brought me way down through Florida to my
next preaching place, with hours of pleasant riding
through sunny countryside in the old Buick! It looked
the same and I felt like kissing it! If it could talk we
would have reminisced all day! It purred along as it used
to do and acted as though it knew the significance of this
day. I rode with mixed emotions, in the front seat as
always, but with a tug at my heart because Sara was no
longer beside me. For over two years I have lived in that
awareness. I'm not getting used to it—just learning to
live with it.

It is a wonder how inanimate things can take on so
much meaning by reason of the memories that make
them precious. I live in an apartment full of them and
have no desire to leave it although loneliness sometimes

settles deep and dark. Some who are left alone find it unbearable and resort to many desperate measures to break the power of loneliness. But that need not be. I have not lost Sara and these trinkets and treasures keep me company until we meet again. The old Buick won't make it but we will; and if in the world to come, when Jesus reigns over a redeemed earth, we can recover anything of what we once possessed, I'd like to resurrect the old Buick like they reactivate the old car models these days. Then with Sara at the wheel, we'd have a spin down some good road in Kingdom Come!

Just before I left Florida these friends who call themselves the *Keepers of the Buick* brought it to my last preaching place. I saw it standing there as I walked along the street. It seemed the next thing to Sara herself showing up again! The old Buick has done things for me on this trip it never did before. It has made me aware of the nearness of that other world and perhaps the nearness of those who dwell there—nearer than we may know. Let the theologians argue the matter, but I do know that actually I have had a little postscript to remind me that I have not closed the book but only a chapter of a blessed relationship that budded here, to bloom forever in a better climate later on.

23

God of the Valleys

In the twentieth chapter of First Kings we read that the Syrian army was defeated by the soldiers of Ahab, King of Israel. The servants of Benhadad of Syria explained it by saying, "The Israelites worship the god of the hills. If we fight them in the valley we shall overcome them." But a prophet of God said to Ahab, "Because the Syrians say I am a god of the hills but not of the valleys, I will overcome them and we'll know who is God around here!" (*See* 1 Kings 20:23, 28.)

There is a precious lesson hidden in this account. As Christians we are inclined to worship only the God of the hills. We think of Him only in terms of the high and exalted experiences of life, the mountain peaks and heights of glory bright. But He is also the God of life's valleys, dark and trying days when the sun does not shine, when the journey is lonely and painful. Some of life's greatest victories are won in the valleys and not on the mountain tops. If we are hill Christians all the time, trying to live on spiritual excitements, flitting from one thrill to another, building tabernacles on the peaks as Peter wanted to do on the Mount of Transfiguration, we shall certainly be overcome by the enemy. We must know the God of the valleys as well as the God of the peaks. Where there are mountains there must be valleys and we had better be prepared for both. The Christian life is up and down, visions and valleys. Paul dropped all the way from third heaven to the thorn in the flesh to learn that God's grace is sufficient for depth as well as height. Satan's strategy is to defeat us in the lowlands.

Job was a righteous man, faithful in his religious observances, while prosperity smiled upon him in the hills of success, but when he sat in desolation—family gone, possessions gone, health gone and a wife saying, "Curse God and die"—it was then that he took a postgraduate course getting acquainted with the God of the valleys.

John the Baptist could stand on Jordan and shout his bold faith in Jesus Christ but John the Baptist in jail fell so low that he inquired, ". . . Art thou he that should come, or do we look for another?" (Matthew 11:3).

One grows a little suspicious of these souls who say they never doubt or fear, who walk in triumph without ever a defeat, who look with condescending scorn on less radiant saints playing in a minor key. Somehow it is often the very people who boast of highest exaltation and loftiest ecstasies who go down quickly in ignominious defeat. They are not geared for low elevations and need a faith that will not shrink when pressed by many a foe.

Doctor Torrey used to say that those who think they have attained some sublime height of faith and trust, because they never know any agony of conflict or of prayer, have surely gotten beyond their Lord and the mightiest victors for God. There is a *fight* of faith as well as a *rest* of faith, and your knowledge of God is inadequate for life's storm and stress if you know only the

God of the hills. He is the same God as the God of the valleys. Blessed is the man who has found that neither hill nor valley, neither height nor depth, can separate us from His love.

24

"Out of" or "About"

Today I received a letter from a dear soul whose husband died recently. She had read my little book *Though I Walk Through the Valley,* and she said, "You wrote *out of* your experience, not *about it* as so many do." In that one sentence she summed up, with great insight, what makes real Christian testimony. All of us have heard or read accounts of the trials and testings of many people. They fall into two categories: some merely recite what happened—all that one gets is facts and figures—while others pour out their hearts. That is such a different thing from getting things off one's chest! One can read between the lines, and what he reads opens a greater world than pen can reveal or tongue can describe.

Too much Gospel testimony, preaching, writing, and singing suffer from being *about* and not *out of.* It is *about* Jesus, who He was, what He said and did. Sometimes it is a recount of experiences but the spirit is lost in the letter. Deep does not call unto deep. A great preacher asked the soloist of the morning service, "Did you sing from your heart or was it just a song?" On a television program I heard Pablo Casals say to a young cellist who had played, it seemed to me, superbly, "You are playing the notes but not the music." The rendition was flawless technically but the maestro said it wasn't music. I have heard sermons like that and so have you. Everything was "faultily faultless, icily regular, splendidly null." Everything was correct but it was *about* and not *out of*.

> Thy soul must overflow
> If thou another soul would reach;
> It takes the overflowing heart
> To give the lips full speech.

In my days of deepest grief most of the comfort books I read did not comfort. They were *about* sorrow, suffering, and bereavement but not written *out of* it. Whoever wrote about the valley had not been through it. The platitudes were correct, the counsel was sound, but it was notes without music. Sometimes the least gifted soul who couldn't even put it into words gave me a look and a handshake that spoke volumes. The rich young ruler knew all the rules but he wouldn't play the game. His knowledge was *about* but not *out of*. Travelers through these lowlands need more than a road map. Our Lord did not furnish charts, He said, "I am the Way . . ." (John 14:6). He was touched with a feeling of our infirmities and was tempted in all points like as we are. He had been there and He did not speak *about* His experience but *out of* it. The psalmist said, "Thy statutes have been

my songs in the house of my pilgrimage" (Psalms
119:54). When God's law book becomes our song book
and we speak not *about* but *out of* what we have learned,
then we have words *and* music.

25

God's Extras

There is only one Christian life and that is Christ Himself who is the Life. He lives that life again in every
heart that receives Him. What we call the Christian life
is our Lord being Himself in us. As we trust and obey
Him He makes Himself at home in our hearts. We are
not robots, but, as we consent and cooperate, He releases
His power and reveals His presence. "And God is able
to make all grace abound toward you; that ye always
having all sufficiency in all things, may abound to every
good work" (2 Corinthians 9:8). That means that there
will always be enough of all that we need to do, all that
God wants us to do, as long as He wants us to do it.

Just as loving parents provide for their children, so
does our Heavenly Father provide for those who trust,
love, and obey Him. "The Lord is my shepherd; I shall
not want" (Psalms 23:1). But there are extra blessings
which we may have over and above our regular needs if

we but ask for them. When I was a boy, I was lovingly cared for, and, although we were poor, my needs were met from day to day. But there were other extra good things which I wanted, and if my parents thought they were worthwhile, they were granted; however, they would not have known that I wanted them nor would I have received them if I had not asked for them.

The Bible tells us that "we have not because we ask not." (*See* James 4:2.) There are many added blessings that could be ours. We live without them because we do not ask and receive. I am convinced that our Father would grant us far more than our daily requirement of grace if we came boldly to His throne to receive it. "O what peace we often forfeit, O what needless pain we bear—all because we do not carry everything to God in prayer!" Who knows how many might be healed if they, believing, asked for it in faith? It is not always God's will to heal but many a divine touch is missed because we ask not.

Do not be satisfied with the daily run of average requirements. There are extras, for our Father's storehouse is well stocked and the cupboard will never be bare. He is pleased to have us ask for special favors. We honor Him when we expect great things from Him. He is able to do exceeding abundantly above all that we ask or think.

His love has no limit, His grace has no measure,
His power no boundary known unto men;
For out of His infinite riches in Jesus
He giveth and giveth and giveth again.

Shame on us that we live on less than is ours for the asking!

Even among us mortals down here we have bonuses, and the worker sometimes receives extra pay from the boss. Surely our Heavenly Father is not a hard master, doling out bare necessities. He is our *Father* and delights to make glad the hearts of His children. We are not to love Him for His gifts. Be not afraid to ask for more than our daily allowance. There is more, much more, in His abundance that could be ours, but we have not because we ask not. Don't miss God's extras!

26

"Backtracking"

This week I am staying in a motel where there are few opportunities for quiet walking. The best escape from streets and traffic I can find is an old deserted railroad track, overgrown with weeds, that leads through the bushes and ends at nowhere. The rusty and rotting rails and cross-ties are still there but no trains ride them any more. I am walking back into yesterday and memories of a day forever gone.

I had hoped that America would grow weary of jets and the nightmare of the highway and resurrect train travel. They can do it in Japan and in Europe but we are too far gone for such a life pattern here. We think we are sophisticated but we are really sick. We have stepped up life's tempo to a weird and wild crescendo and we must be from here to yonder at maniac speed, not even stopping to wonder what on this earth is important enough to travel 600 miles-an-hour to reach.

My tramp down the old railroad tracks was backtracking into memory lanes to when I used to crisscross the country by train with time to look out the window and see the landscape instead of gazing at oceans of clouds. Part of the joy of the journey used to be the delight of getting there.

With me rode Sara who loved the trains and to whom a cross-country, three-day trip to California was an anticipated adventure. To sit together in our apartment, shut in from everybody, but with the windows open to the passing scene all became impossible when Progress drove us to air travel and we joined, by compulsion, the jet set.

Then Sara went to heaven, and now I trudge along an old track worn and spent like myself. I am not yet out of commission and I try to keep my rails shining and the cross-ties in repair. But the worn old trail speaks of tender memories and a day when life was simpler and gentler. It reminds me of the old paths where lie the good way and rest for the soul.

They say that a wave of nostalgia is moving among us. I am not surprised, for I can understand how a generation that has fed itself on every thrill and is gorged with the fleshpots of Egypt might well have nausea and turn any direction to escape the utter boredom of the Age of Ennui. I begin to encounter a few meditating strollers who appear to be looking for something or someone that recalls better days—when we didn't know what we had until we lost it. That haunting look on many a face means a longing to retrace steps we took all too lightly in a day past. Somewhere back up the road, we lost something, and no substitute makes up for it. Happy is he who treads the old path of faith and does not have to mourn a day forever gone but looks to a time, soon to break, when all he lost will be regained and an eternity besides!

27

A Charleston Snapshot

Back in 1972, Sara and I spent a happy week in Charleston, South Carolina, while I filled a preaching engagement at the old First Baptist Church, my pastorate for five years, 1934–1939. We strolled around in the delightful old city where I had spent many precious hours as a bachelor preacher long ago.

Down on the Battery, the waterfront, I snapped a picture of Sara. It was May and Charleston was never lovelier. The undeveloped negative of that snapshot lay in the film roll for a year and a half. In the meantime, my dear one went home to heaven. Four months later I had the pictures developed. I was afraid they might not be good after such a long delay, but the snapshot of Sara was clear and in color. Somehow of all the pictures I have gathered since my beloved went away, it has touched me most. It was like coming back from another world. I had only the memory of that sweet morning, but the picture turned memory into reality. There stood Sara with that same dear smile that gladdened my heart for thirty-three years.

But there was more. Reflection brought to my heart not only memory of the past but prospect for the future. Just as in the film negative Sara had lain hidden in the camera for a year and a half, so now her dear body lies in a little Quaker graveyard. One of these days [God hasten it!], the Almighty will open the grave and the *negative* will suddenly become a *positive!* My beloved will rise in a new body transformed by resurrection power, lovelier beyond fondest dreams. I, too, shall be changed, whether dead or living, and in a redeemed earth perhaps, reunited never to separate we shall stroll again in some of the favored spots we enjoyed so much before.

It is not just the dream of a bereaved and weary heart. It is a glorious certainty with the Word of God to guarantee it. Let scoffers sneer and unbelievers scorn, I rest on the promise of Jesus Christ who said, ". . . If it were not so, I would have told you . . ." (John 14:2). I am not interested in quibbling about the recognition of loved ones in the world to come. I know there is not much Scripture dealing expressly with it. Is it not because it is so perfectly obvious and God expects us to take it for granted? It has been said many times that surely we shall not know less in the hereafter than we know now. Anything less than glad reunion is utterly unthinkable.

Just because we do not marry in heaven does not mean

that the saints are reduced to a dull uniformity where one is no more precious to us than another. I shall look for Sara and she will not be lost in the anonymity of a faceless multitude, all looking exactly alike. Our poor minds can conjure up problems on the subject, but my Father will have worked it all out in infinitely more joy—certainly not less—than we knew down here.

I await the day when all the *negatives*—and some were in a sad state when we laid them away—will be developed into glorious *positives* [not pictures but persons], and we shall see smile again those faces that we have loved long since and lost awhile. God will not fill countless hearts through the centuries with an unutterable longing only to dash those hopes to the ground without fulfillment.

So I lovingly fondle my little picture that says so much, far beyond itself, about one now removed but one day to be restored.

28

I'll Soon Find Out!

A thousand questions come to mind when one reaches the mid-seventies as is my case, both in this century and in my own life span. I was born in 1901 and am therefore always a year behind in the 1900's. I have had my threescore and ten, and now a five-year bonus has been added.

There are many in my bracket. Senior citizens have set a statistical record lately. Many have made it into the nineties, and there are a few centenarians around. Now, in the seventies, there are already many years behind us and our twenties seem like antiquity!

I'm nearer to my heavenly home than I've ever been before. Some oldsters try not to think about the future and try all sorts of tricks and devices to keep from facing reality. I draw near to the next world with keen interest and high expectation. There is only one authoritative textbook on the subject, my Bible. Almost all of my family have gone across to the other side and I eagerly seek all the light I can get on how they do over there. There are not many Scriptural details about it and I would not build a doctrine out of wishful thinking without support in the Book. There are speculations aplenty and I am consumed with curiosity. God has not told us all we would like to know. One thing is certain, I don't have long to wait until Jesus comes or I go. What lies beyond will not lie in mystery much longer. I'll soon find out what it is like and I will have all eternity to explore!

On lonely walks or in the stillness of midnight I am so aware that I see through a glass darkly. God has said enough to whet our appetites and He made it clear, ". . . if it were not so, I would have told you . . ." (John 14:2). He leaves the impression that we can take much for granted on the basis of what we are already guaranteed. God gives us credit for enough common sense to fill in the gaps until faith gives way to sight.

I marvel at the lackluster dullness of so many Christians who plod along as though the life to come were a fairy tale—at best only a hope. I am constantly amazed that churches full of people sit blandly through the preaching and singing about what lies beyond as though it were only something pretty to think about but not really certain. Have we heard about it too much and for too long? Let someone precious to us leave for that world and we may perk up momentarily with a concern that was mildly casual in other days.

What do they look like? What do they think? How will we relate when next we meet? Do they see us now? These and countless other mysteries fill our thoughts many a lonely hour. We can only leave it with our Father. He will take care of it all in a way beyond our fondest imaginings. Meanwhile, we must not sit day-dreaming. There is work to do. Whatever lies out there—farther along we'll know all about it.

I'll soon find out!

29

Home Before Dark

I have been intrigued by the title of a fine book about the hereafter. It reads, *Home Before Dark*. When I was a little boy, it was an unwritten law of the Medes and Persians that I should always be home before dark. No exceptions, no argument. Father and I didn't dialogue much in those days!

Now I'm at the other end of my life span and I still want to get home before dark in more ways than one. For one thing, I pray it will be before dark comes in the loss of my faculties so that I become a helpless vegetable like the sad sights I see in some homes for the aged—poor hunks of flesh kept going by machines that prolong death instead of life. I have no control over such a possibility, but I'd like to go home before that dark sets in.

I want to go home before the dark when I can no longer preach. "I must work the works of him that sent me, while it is day: the night cometh, when no man can work" (John 9:4). Samuel Johnson carried a watch with an inscription inside that read THE NIGHT COMETH.

Doctor William Culbertson of Moody Bible Institute cherished a poem by John Oxenham which ran like this:

> Lord, when Thou seest that my work is done,
> Let me not linger on,
> With failing powers,
> Adown the weary hours,—
> A workless worker in a world of work.
> But, with a word,
> Just bid me home,
> And I will come
> Right gladly,—
> Yea, right gladly
> Will I come.

I want to go home before dark, before some big blunder on the home stretch, some tragic mistake in old age, whether within or beyond my control, which everyone, forgetful of all the good things of the years before, would remember. There is no fool like an old fool. I remember the prayer of one dear saint, "Lord, keep me from becoming a wicked old man!" Christians are saved but never safe so far as witness and example are concerned, never until we reach heaven. The bark can perish in the haven's mouth!

I want to go home before darkness settles on this world. The lights are going out everywhere these days. It is the darkness that precedes the dawn.

> Abide with me, fast falls the eventide;
> The darkness deepens; Lord, with me abide.
>   HENRY F. LYTE

Like the weary disciples on the road to Emmaus, I would say, "Lord, it is toward evening and the day is far spent" (*see* Luke 24:29), not only the day of my life but the day of this age. Be not only Guest but Host at my table and make Thyself known in the breaking of the bread.

O. Henry, the famed short-story writer, uttered as his last words, "I don't want to go home in the dark." Neither do you nor I! I want to make it to that better land of which I read, ". . . there shall be no night there" (Revelation 21:25).

Whatever you do, make sure that you get home before it is dark, while the day of grace is still yours. When that day passes, it will be too late. "Judas went out . . . and it was night" (John 13:30). The soul that departs from Jesus Christ always walks into the night.

Get home before dark!

30

Go Home and Tell

For Sara and me 1973 opened with great promise. Everything looked like a happy old age together. Circumstances smiled upon us. We lived in a lovely new apartment. We were ready to buy a new car. We had enjoyed a delightful trip to Europe and the Holy Land. The preaching itinerary for 1973 was most inviting.

Then everything collapsed. I sat for six months by Sara's bedside and watched her die in a futile and frustrating battle with a weird ailment still baffling to medicine and a mystery to me.

Should I leave the apartment, so fragrant with its memories, and spend my last days in a new place? With my reflective habits and remembering past years when insomnia plagued me, I considered the angles. At first I was sore beset and I used some of the sedatives the doctor prescribed. Then I set the bottle of pills aside and asked the Lord to give His beloved sleep. He did and I decided to stay right in the familiar rooms loaded with things we had so lately bought and planned to enjoy together. You cannot run from life by leaving the scenes of sad experiences. The place to win the victory is *here* and the time is *now*. If we cannot triumph today where we are, we shall not come off conqueror wherever we

may go. There have been dark moments and long hours
of floor walking, sometimes longing for the touch of the
vanished hand and the sound of the voice now still. But
the very setting has helped us gather the treasures of
darkness, to write and preach with a new note that has
brought letters and calls from other beleaguered souls
everywhere saying, "You have helped."

We must all contend with the urge to get away from
where we are to the next pasture where the grass looks
greener. This is a day of two-year preachers who cannot
stay anywhere long enough to build an enduring edifice.
The work is too hard, the wife is unhappy, the weather is
bad, so whether the reason be the church, the companion, or the climate, away they go!

One thinks of the demoniac whom Jesus healed. He
wanted to join the Saviour's evangelistic party. What an
addition he would have been! Up to that time disciples
had been fishermen, tax collectors, an ordinary assort-
ment of rookies nobody would have looked at twice.
Think what an ex-demoniac would have done to perk up
such a team! People would have come from miles around
to see a converted wild man!

But our Lord told him to go back home and bear his
witness there. No more uninviting place could be im-
agined. How would his old friends receive him?
Wouldn't it be wiser to take a new start somewhere else?
I am glad that he obeyed the Lord and did as he was told.
It is a temptation to hide from life, nursing our sorrow
and reading devotional books, but we have business to
attend to. This man longed to stay close to Jesus in per-
son but his job was to go and represent Jesus to many
persons. And there is no better place to start than at
home.

31

From Myrtles to Blackpolls

Today I heard my first myrtle warbler of the season. How welcome is his jingle and what a pretty sight he is among the earliest blossoms! He leads the procession of warblers and the blackpoll brings up the rear in late spring. There is an all-too-brief span of a few precious weeks between myrtles and blackpolls. I look forward to that interim between winter and summer. Why can't this season be as long as winter, interminable winter that reigns like a tyrant over almost half of the year? In these few weeks the warbler wave passes through. Some stay to nest and rear their young, others are simply transients heading north. One is almost overwhelmed by them while they last. Then one day we hear the musical castanets of the blackpoll and we know the caravan has passed.

Just the same, it is worth the long wait to see the myrtle warblers in the trees, just as the robin's song is worth months of winter. By the time they arrive, the appetite has been whetted to a fine point and fond anticipation has reached its peak. Whether or not the realization is worth the long anticipation raises an age-old question that covers a thousand other things.

This morning I heard a yellow warbler at a distance.

What a golden sprite of springtime he is! Then there are the goldfinches and purple finches chattering in the trees. The chipping sparrow is here, of course, a plain little gentleman with a simple chip and a bit of a trill. Chippies are just plain folks and they add a wholesome balance to the bird picture along with their more glamorous and colorful fellows.

I have never known what to call myself as to my interest in birds. I detest the terms *bird lover* and *bird watcher*. The first is too sentimental and the second suggests a pop-eyed freak staring up at the trees, the butt of so many jokes. I am certainly not an ornithologist and to say *bird man* suggests a man who looks like a bird. All I can say is, "You name it!"

It is difficult to find a kindred spirit with an eye and ear for birds. If I say that I want to get outdoors, some dear soul takes me for a ride, which is not at all what I had in mind. If once in a long while some well-meaning friend goes with me for a walk he talks when I want to be still. In the thirty years that I have been a traveling preacher I have not found a dozen men who know or care anything about songbirds. A few rare souls speak the language and finding one is like finding a brother of some secret order or meeting an American in a foreign land. Immediately we begin to share our experiences, and the uninitiated look on in uncomprehending silence.

Is it not the same with the Christian fellowship? Many can talk for hours on other subjects, some can *talk church* but how few belong to the fellowship of those who, like God's people in Malachi's day, feared the Lord and spake often one to another? (*See* Malachi 3:16.) This is not the same as a lot of chatter at a church social along

with the coffee and cake. These are sharers of another
life who speak another language. Most church members
can speak it only in broken phrases, like a foreigner who
has learned a few sentences in English. That blessed
company who know Him, the power of His Resurrection,
and the fellowship of His sufferings, know each other
when they meet and never tire of talking about Him
whom having not seen they love.

32

The Puzzle-Picture

All afternoon Johnny tried to put together his puzzle-
picture birthday gift from his father. But, try as he would,
nothing came of it. Some of the pieces were bright, some
dark, some seemed to fit nowhere. Finally in his frustra-
tion he gathered the whole mixture into the box and gave
it to his dad. "I can't do it," he explained. "You try it." Of
course Father assembled it in a few minutes. "You see,"
he said, "I knew what the picture was like all the time. I
saw the picture in the puzzle, you saw only the pieces."

God has a plan for our lives. To us, so much that happens seems to fit nowhere, makes no sense. The more we
try to get things together, the more they fall apart. It is
not in man that walketh to direct his steps or to arrange
the pieces of his life. But because they make no sense to
us does not mean that they make no sense. Because they

make no sense now does not mean that they never will make sense. Because they make no sense to us does not mean that they make no sense to God. It will be a great day for any man when he gathers up all the segments of his life and hands them over to God. We see through a glass as in a riddle and we see only the pieces and the puzzle. God sees the picture.

We are told that all things work together for good—those are the pieces—to those called according to God's purpose—that is the picture. Whether or not we let God assemble the pieces determines whether it shall be a picture or only a puzzle. Are you perplexed and frustrated over this event or that happening in your life? Do not take it out of God's hand to work it into your design. God saw the picture from the start and you don't see it yet and won't until it is finished. When Joseph was sold into Egypt his father said, ". . . all these things are against me" (Genesis 42:36). So it *seemed* to him. But later Joseph said to his brothers, ". . . ye thought evil against me: but God meant it unto good . . ." (Genesis 50:20). That is how it *was* with God.

Sometimes, flat on our backs in a hospital or grieving at a grave, we wrestle with one big dark piece of the puzzle. We cannot imagine how this could be part of a beautiful picture. Some things are Satan's doing and some are our clumsy mistakes. The Scriptures give credit where it is due. Paul's thorn in the flesh was the messenger of Satan. But even the grievous tragedies of God's men find a place in His overall purpose. Some pieces are not good but they work together for good in the total picture.

Just gather up the whole jumble and lay it at His feet.

Consent to His purpose and cooperate with it. One day the picture will be unveiled.

> Not now, but in the coming years,
> It may be in the better land,
> We'll read the meaning of our tears,
> And there, sometime, we'll understand.
>   MAXWELL CORNELIUS

Remember, now you see the puzzle but God sees the picture. Don't get lost among the pieces!

33

"Awake, Dear?"

Through thirty-three years on the road we stayed in motels. Countless times across those years I would call in a whisper from my bed to hers, "Awake, Dear?" Sometimes the night was long or pressing cares bothered my afternoon nap. I wanted to talk something over—or just talk.

This is not a lament about the unutterable loneliness since she went away. It would take a shelf of volumes to record how I miss her. It is rather a question aimed now not at the other side of a room but at another world on the other side of this life. She has gone there to be with Christ and I do not know much about it. I know that it is far, *far* better and I would not bring her back to this wretched world and her bed of pain.

> How happy are the saints above
> Who once went sorrowing here!
> But now they taste unmingled love
> And joy without a tear.
>
> THOMAS SHEPHERD

But I read that she sleeps in Jesus and that raises questions. I do not buy soul-sleeping. Paul would not have longed to depart and be with Christ if it had meant centuries of unconsciousness. Why hurry? My Lord said, ". . . To day shalt thou be with me in paradise" (Luke 23:43). My dear one sleeps in Jesus, a figure of rest from all she suffered here. But we are not unconscious when we sleep. We dream and can be awakened.

So I call gently sometimes in the night, "Are you awake, Dear?" Does she know that I call? Does she know how it is with me these days? But you say she might worry about me if she did. No, she sees from God's side, and if we could see as God sees, there would be no grief. She knows how everything really is, not just how it seems to be. Nothing distresses her now.

She is awake over there. But I cannot see that world with these eyes. I can only dream and hope and believe. I see through a glass as in a riddle. There is no answer now as I lie alone, in old age back to the life of a loner as it was before I knew her. This is only an interruption, an interval. The end of the chapter reads "to be continued." I am human and the heart is lonely. She is not in the next bed but maybe nearer than the next bed! I'll make it through long nights and lonely days until these times be past. And it helps to whisper at two in the morning, "Awake, Dear?"

Only those who long for a vanished hand and the sound of a voice that is still understand all this. From the rest it brings only an uncomprehending smile, a tolerance but not participation. I do not blame them. I was like that too. You have to be there to know how it is. You have to belong to the club. Then it means something to awaken at midnight and whisper, "Awake, Dear?"

34

Christmas Again

One more Christmas and, as submerged in commercialism as we may be, I am still thankful that I am in a land where I can hear the carols. Uncounted millions in Russia, China, and other lands will not hear "Silent Night" and "Hark! the Herald Angels Sing." I deplore the takeover by the hucksters and Santa Claus. This may not be the day my Lord was born but I find Him amidst all the hoopla that even the church mixed with paganism long ago, according to Augustine. I do not find Him in the hoopla but in my heart.

Last night we drove through a residential section of our city, and the streets were lined with candles in paper bags partly filled with sand. I shall have to borrow two overworked words from the parlance of today to say it was positively beautiful and fantastic—rows of soft lights in the darkness transforming the neighborhood into a fairyland. Preacher that I am, I could not miss the lesson in it. What could be plainer and simpler than paper bags, sand, and little candles? Christians are the light of the world, and if only we could let our lights truly shine, this city would be aglow and men would glorify our Father in heaven. It does not require Hollywood glamour, extravaganzas, or even theologians, but just plain Christians being what they are.

We are obsessed with the delusion that we must copy the world and stage spectaculars and make the Gospel a form of entertainment. The early church did not dramatize it, they declared it by life and lip as sons of God in the midst of a crooked and perverse nation, among whom they shone as lights in the world. They lit up the Roman Empire with their testimony and some of them did it with their burning bodies. We still sing:

> Our fathers, chained in prisons dark,
> Were still in heart and conscience free:
> How sweet would be their children's fate,
> If they, like them, could die for Thee!

But later versions have toned down that verse in keeping with our modern comfortable Christianity.

Last night I had a little prayer in Sara's room. Four years ago I went into that room to say, "You're my Christmas." This is my third Christmas without her. This is the hardest time of year to get through when half of me is gone. But God has compensated with unnumbered blessings and there are a thousand memories. How they linger!

The news reports this morning do not sound like peace on earth, goodwill to men, or even among men of goodwill, if you like it that way. Well, it didn't look so good long ago in Bethlehem. But God started something then and He is going to see it through. He who was a Babe in Bethlehem is coming back, and more dear souls than you might think are not only waiting but watching for His return. Here again the candles and paper bags come in. The church is not a little club with its main business now for its members to sit tight and hold hands until Jesus comes. We ought to light our candles after we get them out from under the bushels and the beds and let them shine, not to blind people with a glare, but just to bless people with a glow.

If we ever do that, every day will be Christmas just as every day for a Christian ought to be Easter and Thanksgiving!

35

"The Patience of Unanswered Prayer"

Countless are the books on prayer. We are told that God always answers prayer, sometimes saying *no*, sometimes *yes*, sometimes *wait*, but always He answers. However, the third category, when He says *wait*, may include those petitions when we seem to get no answer at all. Perhaps there is a fourth classification: those prayers that seem to bring no response whatever. It was this kind that gave us the line in that precious hymn "Spirit of God, Descend Upon My Heart" that prays a prayer itself when it says, "Teach me the patience of unanswered prayer."

Whether we like it or not, there come those times when the heavens seem brass, when we see only the cold law of cause and effect. ". . . all things continue as they were from the beginning of the creation" (2 Peter 3:4). So say the scoffers about our Lord's return but they say it about other matters too. We pray and nothing happens. Silence. There is no breakthrough. No angel visitant when we beckon. There is neither *yes* nor *no*, just nothing. God seems to have forgotten us. A definite *no* would be more welcome. At least it would settle things!

Such times call for patience as the hymn declares, "the patience of unanswered prayer." Patience to wait, to be faithful, to carry on, feel like it or not, when nothing happens that cannot be explained by natural causes. A sense of things real comes doubly strong and heaven is far away. We read and hear glowing accounts of Divine intervention but it happened to somebody else. To live success when it looks like failure, to sing when we sigh within, to endure as seeing Him who is invisible—not really seeing but as though we saw Him—that calls for the patience of unanswered prayer.

I rejoice to hear in meetings thrilling recitals of deliverance, healing, guidance, and revival. But sometimes I feel that the greatest hero of faith in the meeting may be some humble soul who has no glamorous story to relate but is true anyhow, believing without seeing. And

". . . blessed are they that have not seen, and yet have believed" (John 20:29). Peter heard His Lord say that and wrote later, ". . . in whom, though now ye see him not, yet believing, ye rejoice with joy unspeakable and full of glory" (1 Peter 1:8). That is it, the faith that is not conditioned on seeing. Such is the patience of unanswered prayer.

Like Paul in the storm at sea, we can say, "I believe God" even though it may not look like God is around. Paul did not just believe about God or in God, he believed God. He had God's word for it and so have we. And that word must tide us over those times when He does not speak. There may be times when He seems, as Jeremiah put it in chapter fifteen, verse 18, "as a liar and as waters that fail." But we can remember times when He did answer and the many times He has answered others. We are never walking more surely by faith than when all we have for the moment is His word. In such cases He has already answered before we asked. On that we must rest until He speaks again. There is more to that line in the hymn with which we began: "Teach me . . . to check the rising doubt, the rebel sigh." The best cure for that is "the patience of unanswered prayer"!

36

Stroller in Snow

I shouldn't have done it. Such is the consensus of caution. It was snowing vigorously and I donned my snow-walking gear in a hurry and got into a patch of woods just across the street on the University campus. Oldsters in their mid-seventies should not do such capers, they said, I might break a leg or hip or catch my death of cold! For me there should be only cozy nooks, well warmed, where I could look out the window and let it go at that. But away I went and how I loved it! I came back and read a thing I wrote thirty years ago when I took another stroll in the snow back in the hills. That many years make a difference but the zest is still there, and I am amazed at how well my legs and breath hold up.

In this synthetic, computerized age a walk in snowy woods is at least a short respite from the colorless, drab existence we now call progress. It seems we left behind us when we got into this mess the thing we've been trying to find ever since. There are ski resorts now and a new world of artificial excitement, but the soul longs for just a plain simple walk all alone in the snow.

Charles A. Lindbergh lamented that he had lived to

see the science he worshipped and the aircraft he loved destroying the civilization we expected them to serve. Lewis Mumford bemoaned the fact that the gods of science have become monsters. Even a short walk in snowy woods and back to things elemental is well worthwhile as a momentary escape from this madhouse we have created.

Our Master set us an example as He walked about in Galilee and talked of birds and flowers and simple things. The gait of Galilee is now out of date in the hustle and bustle of modern Israel. We are even trying to make grown-ups out of teenagers and I have watched children even younger talking ecology on television and a kindergarten class discussing economics! They should be playing hopscotch in the back yard! It is perversion to deny youngsters their childhood. Of such is the kingdom of heaven. We might well sit at their feet sometimes and study their examples.

Who is content nowadays just to stroll in the snow? Even bird watching must be done in a group keeping records of how many saw juncoes and who saw and heard nuthatches! Walking has degenerated into organized hikes.

I came back to read about Theodore Roosevelt who never let the boy in him die and who explored a South American jungle when he was nearly sixty. He never recovered from the rigors of that trip but so what—he *lived* while he was living.

The Christian today is seriously in danger of being pressurized by the tribulations (which really means *pressure*) of this life so that even religious activism smothers reflection and meditation. The average pastor,

dizzy amidst telephones, committee meetings, dead-
lines, and the statistical goals he must reach to keep
status, had better get away somehow or he will end up a
denominational bellhop and ministerial flunkey, overwhelmed with concerns that have little to do with redemption anyway.

I'm glad I walked in the snow. I could have broken a
leg but if I hadn't walked I would almost have had a
broken heart. It is better to take a few risks and live a
little all along than to make an invalid of yourself and
end only with a record of no broken legs!

37

The Vanishing Pedestrian

These are bad days for the pedestrian. A generation on
wheels bent on his extermination bears down upon him.
Americans are not disposed to walk two blocks if trans-
portation is available, and any surviving exception is
stared at as though he were an intruder from Mars.
Policemen keep an eye on any man afoot, suspecting that
he may be up to something. Dogs bark at him as though
an apparition had been sighted. If he is seen strolling
along a highway, it is assumed that he is either out of his
head or out of gas.

Considering the hours Americans sit in cars or offices

all day and stare at television at night, if various parts of
our anatomy develop or degenerate in proportion as they
are used, it will be interesting to see what strange crea-
tures we shall turn out to be in a few decades.

This writer has lived on the road for thirty years and of
necessity, not by choice, stayed in hotels and motels.
These hostelries are not geared to pedestrians. They are
meant for motorists on the move, snatching a few hours'
sleep and a quick meal while they scan road maps figur-
ing out how to get from Dan to Beersheba. Walking is
about as remote to their thinking as space travel to a
Hottentot. I usually find myself in a noisy intersection of
turnpikes, a labyrinth of filling stations, repair shops, and
hamburger stands where walking would mean sudden
death from speeding Jehus who have made highways
more dangerous than battlefields.

Walking implies a degree of solitude and meditation
and this generation is the sworn enemy of both. The
pedestrian is cast upon his resources at both ends, head
and foot. He is obliged to think and walk and many an
American is ill fitted for either. To avoid the necessity of
thinking he carries a transistor radio blaring rock disso-
nance that outscreeches the worst jungle. He avoids a
stroll as he would a plague for he cannot face the suspicious eyes of his contemporaries who wonder what
sinister motives must be behind such strange behavior.

The Bible has a lot to say for the pedestrian. Enoch set
the example. It is said that he walked with God, pleased
God, and was not, for God took him. What a biography
and what an epitaph! Isaac meditated in the fields at
eventide. Our Saviour trod the roads and lakesides of
Galilee. We are bidden to walk as He walked, in new-

ness of life, by faith, worthy of our vocation, cir-
cumspectly, honestly, in light, truth, the Spirit, and love.
Today tourists in the Holy Land rush breathlessly
through Palestine and about all they can say is, "I ran
today where Jesus walked!"

It is general knowledge that walking is the perfect
exercise. Nervous Americans cannot move at that gait so
now we have jogging. Many an illness could be cured if
the patient became a pedestrian.

I anticipate walking on a redeemed earth when the
Saviour returns to set up His kingdom. While I like to
read about the New Jerusalem, I assume that the good
Lord will make ample provision for all who prefer
bypaths to boulevards. The faithful few in Sardis were
promised that they should *walk* with Him in white. God
grant that we shall be qualified to join those purified
pedestrians who will walk with Him there because they
walked with Him here!

38

Since You Went Away

Since you went away, Dear Darling, nothing has been
the same nor will it ever be again. I am not trying to get
over it or used to it, for that is impossible. I am trying to
learn to live with it, for that I must do.

I keep reading your last letter, written before you went
to the hospital, a final reminder of how your faithfulness
carried through to the finish. Sick as you already were—
sicker than you let me know—you had put clean sheets
on my bed, carried out the trash, and tidied up the
apartment. You wanted everything spick and span when
I got home. It always was for thirty-three years and you
weren't about to leave it any other way.

At home or on the road, I'm reminded countless times
a day of all you meant to me and I am heartbreakingly
aware of how I miss you. I arrive at my motel for the
week and almost start to call you before I realize the
phone back home will ring in vain, for there is no cheery
voice to say "Hey, Honey!" I start out to walk, and my
lonely hand instinctively reaches for yours as it always
did when we set out for a stroll to look over some new
place. I stumble down motel steps to the lobby and
breakfast every morning—but what's the use? There'll
be no airmail letter as there always was seven days every
week.

I return from my travels, not home, but to an empty
apartment. I wearily enter and put down my things and a
hundred precious memories surround me. If only you
could come into the kitchen just once more in that red
robe and let me turn down the collar—that always somehow was tucked in—before I kiss you at the start of the
day. On the road I find myself subconsciously looking for
you to come down to go to church [I always went down
ahead and waited]. You always wore a hat whether any
other woman did or not! I find myself at church wearily
looking over the crowd for a face I cannot see. At home
I'd give a lot to see you drive the old Buick in while I

come down to carry in the purchases. Both you and the Buick are gone and only I remain. I can only say with Tennyson:

> But O for the touch of a vanished hand
> And the sound of a voice that is still!

I am carrying on in the way I think you'd have me do. I'm *walking through* the Valley, not *wallowing in* it. I am not sitting up with the past or worshipping at the shrine of the dead. You are still alive—more alive than ever—and you have just gone away, a little ahead. I shall overtake you presently or perhaps we'll meet next at "the Great Getting-Up Morning" when you'll rise first and together we'll meet the Lord in the air. If it were not so He would have told us. Anyway, we have not seen each other for the last time. Christians never meet for the last time!

> And next time it's for ever.
> And you'll never go away!

39

Seekers of Signs

The scribes and Pharisees asked Jesus for a sign, a miracle. He answered that He would give only one sign, His own Resurrection, typified in the experience of Jonah. As He hung on the cross, His enemies said, ". . . let him now come down from the cross, and we will believe him" (Matthew 27:42). Today an adulterous generation still asks for signs and wonders: Show us enough miracles and we will believe.

There were miracles in the Bible and God still performs miracles today but they are not the basis for Christian life and experience. Salvation does not come by the assent of the head but by the consent of the heart. One is not born again when he accepts enough signs and wonders to believe that Jesus is the Saviour of the world but when he trusts Jesus as his own personal Saviour with a simple, childlike trust. The Christian faith is built on the miracle of the Resurrection. We are not saved by intellectually agreeing that Jesus rose from the dead but by receiving the risen Saviour into the heart. The Scriptures read, "That if thou shalt confess with thy mouth the Lord Jesus, and shalt believe in thine heart that God hath raised him from the dead, thou shalt be saved" (Romans 10:9).

In our daily living as Christians, God works through faith and obedience, not by occasional miracles. There may be miracles but these are the exceptions that prove the rule. Too many dear souls would live by fits and starts, signs and wonders, but if everything were miraculously provided, we would need no faith. We live in a world spoiled by sin and subject to all the distempers and accidents and troubles that beset humanity in general. It is a world run largely by the law of cause and effect but the Christian walks by a faith that believes when it cannot see or understand and when no sudden revelation comes to clear away the fog. If God supplied us with instant ready answers to every problem or angel intervention in every crisis, there could be no growth of rugged Christian character in the storms of life. If we must have signs and wonders, then we belong to the adulterous generation that believes only what the senses will accept.

Here lies the answer to why we know so little about our loved ones, now with the Lord, and the conditions of life in the world to come. God has told us only as much as we need, not all that we want to know. Our present faculties could not take it in if we did learn the details of the heavenly world. The present chrysalis is not ready to discover what it means to be a butterfly. We have our Lord's word for it and His experience on both sides of the grave and what the inspired writers have told us must be enough while we make our way by faith and not by sight.

This present generation is fed up with amazing marvels and children have grown up watching atomic bombs go off and men walk on the moon. They are bored with what would have been miracles only a few years ago. What do you give a child that would surprise him? An adulterous generation demands that God go into the show business and that Jesus leap from the pinnacle of the temple. But God will not woo us with a bag of tricks, as it were. The way is by faith that cometh by hearing— hearing by the Word of God.

40

Touch Him and Tell It!

Jesus was on His way to the house of Jairus and a crowd of people thronged Him. In the crowd was a poor sick woman, health gone, money gone, who heard that Jesus was passing by. In holy desperation she pressed through the tumult, touched His garment and was healed. Jesus had already passed her by but she overtook Him and that simple touch stopped the procession, detained our Lord on His errand of mercy, and secured a miracle. Two little words in the narrative stand out, *throng* and *touch*. The crowd thronged Him, only one poor woman touched Him in faith and was healed.

We often overlook one point in this story. The crowd was not indifferent, uninterested. They jostled and crowded each other and followed, from a mixture of motives. Many people crowd Jesus, as it were, at church on

Sunday morning, but do not confuse thronging with touching. We shall not carry away His blessing merely by being among those present. There must be a personal touch of faith, however weak and, maybe, with mixed motives, but *touch* Him we must.

This woman knew little about Jesus and knew little of who He was. She had no theological knowledge about Him and her motives were selfish, she wanted healing for herself. But our Lord honored such an approach and the contact of a trembling finger brought a miracle. I am persuaded that no needy soul ever made the slightest gesture toward Jesus in vain. The weakest faith will secure a blessing if it is true faith in *Him*. ". . . him that cometh to me I will in no wise cast out" (John 6:37) is not hedged about with provisos and restrictions. It may be pitifully imperfect but it will do for a start if it follows through.

It did follow through in this case. Our Lord asked, "Who touched me?" and that put the woman on the spot. The response was complete. Fearing and trembling, knowing what was done in her, she came and fell down before Him and told Him all the truth. Those four ingredients add up to a full confession and a public confession and that is required by our Lord. "Whosoever therefore shall confess me before men, him will I confess also before my Father which is in heaven" (Matthew 10:32). He declared, "Whosoever therefore shall be ashamed of me and of my words in this adulterous and sinful generation; of him also shall the Son of man be ashamed, when he cometh in the glory of his Father with the holy angels" (Mark 8:38). Weak and imperfect the faith may be but He expects public confession. The woman in this story may have been nervous, frightened, poorly dressed, and embarrassed before this crowd. Ashamed of herself, yes, but not of Him! We sadly miss the mark in churches today when we do not recognize that if faith is to be vital it must be vocal to the point of confession. We must confess *with the mouth* Jesus as Lord. It must be visible, "before men," it must be audible, "with the mouth," it must be credible, from the heart, if it is to be acceptable.

Do not think you will steal a secret blessing and sneak silently away. And don't be content with thronging Him whom you must touch if you would be whole.

41

Last Run

We used to call it the Carolina Special and many were the times I rode it home to Greensboro on my travels. Sara and I waited many an evening in the terminal at Cincinnati until time to board our Pullman and ride through the mountains to Knoxville and Asheville and on down home. When I was alone it meant I was on my way to meet my beloved and rest a few days from the rigors of itinerating all over the country. But Progress(?) caught up with us and everybody, including ourselves, elected to fly. The old Carolina Special held on valiantly, losing money all the time, but finally succumbed to the new age.

Just a few days ago another old veteran gave up. The Piedmont Limited carried us north or south and we rode it first on our wedding trip heading for New Orleans and then, by Southern Pacific, to California. It meant a long ride through Dixie back when Dixie was Dixie and cotton fields had not yet given way to factories and before the South had become richer in what money can buy and poorer in what it cannot buy.

I didn't feel like going to the station to witness that last trip. I've had enough good-byes lately. There was a good-bye to dear Sara, then to the old Buick we enjoyed so much, to countless plans we had made, and to the prospect of old age together. Old trains develop personalities like old friends, and it wrings the heart to close an era that may not have been as sophisticated and speedy but carried tender associations which this new delirium tremens of jets and computers can't match.

Science, once worshiped as a god, has become a monster. Rabelais said, "Science without conscience is but the ruin of the soul." We are thankful for all the blessings that inventive genius has produced and we do not long to return to dirt roads, kerosene lamps, and the horse-and-buggy days. The tragedy is that man's brain has conjured up a new world which he is not morally capable of handling, and the road to Megalopolis is not going to climax in Paradise but in a Babylon, doomed to destruction.

If we were really going somewhere by changing over, again and again, to more sophisticated living, we might bear the passing of old joys with some satisfaction, but there is not much exhilaration in merely going faster if mankind does not know where it is going.

Thank God, a portion of humanity still believes in God and in His purpose in history. Some of us believe that, when we sit in the shambles of the Tower of Babel created amidst the final confusion of tongues, Jesus Christ will return and take over.

But I still wish I could board the Carolina Special again and take off with my dear one on the Piedmont Limited. We lost something somewhere in the past twenty-five years which smart sophistication has not made up for. We behold a generation that has gained a world and lost its soul.

Like these old trains, we ourselves near the end of our run. We rejoice that the Lord, and not the scientist, is our shepherd. The redemption of men and of creation is in better hands than in the laboratories of mortal men.

42

The Mansion and the Mountains

Although I am a North Carolinian and am now seventy-five years old, yesterday was my first visit to the Biltmore House and Gardens at Asheville. I strolled through the fabulous mansion and viewed the lavish furnishings, the tapestries and paintings, the grand staircase, library, bedrooms, dining rooms, all of them unforgettable in their elegance.

As I walked through all this grandeur, I paused to look out an upstairs window at the autumn woods stretching back to the mountains. What I beheld outside the mansion outclassed all I had seen within. The grounds, the woods in all directions, the mountains in the background—all were at their October peak in colors beyond words. I have seen autumnal beauty these many years in many settings but I have never seen a sight that overcame me as did this sight.

One earlier impression lingers as I have written about it in an earlier book. I was in Geneva, Switzerland, and, as I looked out my hotel window, I saw below the League of Nations building, monument to a dream that failed. Then I lifted my gaze to view, far in the distance, the Alps with Mont Blanc rearing its snow-clad shoulders high above the clouds. The double view symbolized the temporal on one hand and the eternal on the other, man's little day and God's forever, peace palaces that fail and God's mountains that endure while centuries come and go. I had the same feeling when I surveyed the mansion and the mountains: what man can do and what only God can do. Only God can make a tree and assemble millions of them in matchless beauty.

That glory of yesterday's autumnal scene spoke to me of a day to come, intimating how this earth may look when Satan's reign ends and Jesus rules over a redeemed creation. It gives an earnest, a foretaste, of that better day to come when God reclaims and recovers from sin, death, and corruption this poor, blighted planet. That will be the Regeneration, the Restoration, the Redemption now drawing nigh. He is not going to let the devil get away with his usurpation forever. Paradise will be regained. With me it is a favorite dream and it is not a fantasy born of wishful thinking. It is Biblical, made crystal clear in Romans 8 and elsewhere in God's Book. The whole creation stands on tiptoe waiting for that day.

Such glimpses as I had yesterday confirm my conviction that if there can be such beauty in spots even now, in this poor world still in the bondage of corruption, what will it be like when God restores a ruined creation and the saints walk around in it for a thousand years! That opens tantalizing suggestions beyond the limits of this little sketch. I can only thank God for glimpses like yesterday's and such previews from His Word. Help me even now to taste the powers of the Age to Come!

43

Lifetime Semi-Retirement

Down in Georgia, deep in Dixie, I arrived at my motel to find plenty of walking room in the beginnings of a new highway, just a big dirt road, at present, with no traffic. I found myself saying, "Lord, You really didn't have to do all this just to give me a walking place for three days!" I've seen new highway beginnings many times before now, as this itinerant preacher traveled in such spots all over the country for thirty-odd years.

It is early May and down my road I strolled to hear my

spring birds: the indigo bunting, white-eyed vireo, yellow-breasted chat, yellowthroat, prairie warbler, and many more common feathered songsters. How thankful I am that through all these years God has given me a ministry that gives unhurried time to walk, to meditate, and to write. I make my own schedule and report to no office but heaven. I don't have to stay anywhere longer than a week. I try to gather messages that may help others who do not have such a life-style. I belong to no club nor movement and promote nothing except the good news of a Saviour come and a Saviour coming. Such a ministry is not registered in the usual religious catalog. Not many prophets are found in the classified lists of the clergy.

Pastors tell me how churches demand more of one man than most men can do, requiring that he be jack-of-more-trades than ever before; with no time for reflection, in a hectic rat race, so busy doing the wishes of people that there is scant time to do the will of God. Unless the average preacher drastically revises his program, he ends up a frustrated church flunkey.

The average modern man aims at getting in shape for a happy retirement. If he reaches that age he may be too spent in body and mind to enjoy it. I resolved early to take my retirement all along lest it never accumulate for old age. Why not have it in installments now while I have eyes to see and ears to hear, before the years draw nigh when I shall say, "I have no pleasure in them"? If my last day should be today, death will not have cheated me out of what I meant to do and never got around to doing! I've been doing it all along!

Was not this the pattern of my Lord's life-style? If the Son of God, with only three years to preach, and a world to save, could so blend labor and leisure as to find time for fishing, for hours in the mountain, and for meals with Mary, Martha, and Lazarus, who are we to think our work too important to allow such time out! How can we do His work it we do not live His life? It is time to slow down to the gait of Galilee!

Instead of full-time retirement in an old age you may never reach, why not live in part-time retirement now? Can't afford to? Can you afford *not* to? It does not mean quitting what you are doing so much as cultivating a mind and heart at rest so that you can take an *inside vacation* while you work. And check on how you waste the leisure you do have! Don't kill yourself saving up for a day you may never see!

44

"To Finish with the Scroll"

Should you go first and I remain
To finish with the scroll—

Flying toward Arkansas on a lovely afternoon, I am alone, of course. Only those who are truly alone in this world know true loneliness. I have countless friends and some relatives but, without wife or children, the difference is profound. I might as well face it, if I shuffled off this mortal coil today it really wouldn't make much dif-

ference to anybody. I don't blame others. They have
their own lives to live. Things go that way in this world.
I'm not complaining. I detest self-pity and want no sym-
pathy. It is perfectly understandable that we can't stop
long to bemoan anything or anybody for we must get on
with the job.

When my dearest went first and left me to finish with
the scroll, I sought surcease by communicating my grief,
but I soon discovered that in grief is the greatest communication gap of all. It did not take long to find out that
only those who have been there could understand. That
is perfectly normal for others have not sat where I sit.
Dear Billy and Ruth Graham drew near to me and Billy
said, "I haven't been there but as far as I can I want to
feel with you in your grief." That revealed real under-
standing. Through the years I had tried to comfort many
who had lost the other half of their lives but I hadn't
been there.

Even those whose wife or husband has gone the way
of death are not all of them able to be of much help. We
live in a day without natural affection when love is cheap
and shallow. Thousands cannot even wait for death to
part them! And many who have been separated by the
Grim Reaper do not show evidence of a deep wound.
Did they love John or Mary as I loved Sara? This thought
was frustrating and thinned greatly the circle of my comforters.

Then there are Job's comforters of diverse kinds. The
bouncing cheer-'em-upper who has never really had
much trouble but has ready answers for every
question—from such, dear Lord, deliver us! The
academic sort who, when asked about our loved ones
now with Christ and whether they know about us, goes

into a short lecture about the trichotomy of body, soul, and spirit. We are informed that since they are now spirits they have only God-consciousness. Such loads of learned lumber construct poor resting places for bereft mortals who remain to finish with the scroll!

But there are a few dear hearts who have been there. They spin no theories. Sometimes there is only the pressure of a hand, a tear in the eye. It is easy for us out of wishful thinking to develop doctrines about the hereafter that have no support in the Word of God. But there is something that transcends knowledge and some of us feel it without words to say it. The Scriptures do not go into detail about those gone before, but there are intimations that light up our prospects. The crumbs whet our appetite for the cake!

At any rate while we finish the scroll we can sing,

> Does Jesus care when I've said good-bye
> to the dearest on earth to me,
> And my sad heart aches till it nearly breaks—
> Is it aught to Him? Does He see?
> And jubilantly with good authority, we shout,

> *"Oh, yes, He cares—I know He cares—*
> *His heart is touched with my grief;*
> *When the days are weary, the long nights dreary,*
> *I KNOW my Saviour cares."*

That makes all the difference as we finish with the scroll!

One thing I know. I once read of the man who lived beside a river but had little interest in the people on the other side until his daughter moved over there to live. I have lived beside the river many years but this past year

has heightened a thousandfold my concern about the
other side. I cannot put it into words, but there is an
entirely new dimension and a new affinity. Since the
dearest to me of all on earth has changed worlds I am
more attracted to that world than this. I wonder what she
is like, a personality still but without her body. She is not
gone nor is her soul sleeping. I have no present faculties
capable of comprehending that next state any more than
a chrysalis can understand what it is like to be a butterfly.
But I am charmed, intrigued, and fascinated beyond
words over all the possibilities. Paul visited the third
heaven but could not tell us about it. I know that I make
my way through this weal and woe with happier feet
because I have been told enough to know that the sweet
spirit that made life so precious for thirty-three years has
not disappeared but somewhere awaits a glad reunion. I
too will have to be changed into a being suited to that
new realm. The resurrection will ultimately take care of
all that. If I go before my Lord comes, I am sure there
will be communion sweet in the interim before that
great Getting-up Morning.

How deeply we wish sometimes that the barrier between the here and the hereafter could be broken just
long enough for a word or the touch of a hand! We would
need new eyes, new thought patterns, new equipment
for body, mind, and spirit to understand the speech, the
sights, and the sounds of that world. Time and space are
meaningless, matter offers no obstacles. Our resurrected
Lord entered where doors were shut. The prophet
prayed, "O that thou wouldst rend the heavens and that
thou wouldest come down . . . !" (Isaiah 64:1). He
longed for broken barriers! God has broken them before

now, in His Book, in His Son, in His Spirit, in twice-born people, in answered prayer, and in revival. He will break the barrier when He gathers His church, when Jesus comes to reign. Death breaks it. I am never far from the other world and its people. Whether they come soon with the Lord or I join them beforehand, sometimes it is hard to wait for the Broken Barrier!

Nothing can ever make me believe that the thirty-three happy years with my beloved can be forever terminated by the rude hand of death, never to be continued somewhere under better conditions. Satan cannot have the last word and though death is the last enemy to be destroyed, his doom is certain. I am distinctly told that in heaven we neither marry nor are given in marriage but are as the angels—not angels but like the angels—in that the marriage relationship will not be continued. That does not mean that the special love we had for each other down here will be obliterated and one will be as near to us as another. God will not discontinue love as precious as that, letting us lift that cup to our lips here, only to have it forever dashed to the ground. Nothing as sweet as that is doomed to end with a casket and a grave, put away in a box in a hole in the ground, a brutal ending in devilish glee to an angelic story that started in heaven. God and not the devil is on the throne and so:

Yet Love will dream and Faith will trust,
Since He Who knows our need is just,
That somehow, somewhere, meet we must . . . .
That life is ever lord of death,
And love can never lose its own!

JOHN GREENLEAF WHITTIER

45

Songs in Winter

On a wintry morning the birds are few and my appreciation is whetted all the more for the hardy remnant that did not go South at the first chilly blast of late autumn. I respect them for staying with me through these bleak months. Whatever the travel folders say, it seems as though North Carolina these days has six months of winter and two weeks of spring. It wouldn't be so bad if winter could give up and spring dared to come, but by the time the transition is really made, it is almost summer.

I am thankful for the cheerful chickadees who stay in good humor come wind, come storm. The saucy titmouse shouts, "Peto, peto," as if daring the elements. The tiny kinglets thrive in a temperature that sends me indoors. The nuthatches explore the tree trunks head downward and the brown creeper investigates head upward so between them the woods get a going over from the ground up and from the top down. The woodpeckers are doing a brisk business, and the juncoes make me feel that a snow is coming.

The starlings, for all their bad reputation, are not entirely unwelcome. They are here and common misery makes strange company acceptable. We are all prisoners of winter so we develop a sort of comradeship during our incarceration.

This morning I heard a starling imitating a wood pewee so perfectly that I could have shut my eyes and thought I was in the woods in mid-summer. He is not fooling me, however, for I am aware of his old tricks. There are some mockingbirds around but they have no remarks to make and on a morning like this I don't blame them. It is strictly "no comment" as far as they are concerned. The bluejays are as noisy as ever and their screeching discord seems sharpened by the freezing winds.

When winter comes I spend the first months in a sort of dull resignation. Spring seems so distant that I cannot even raise a feeble hope. By the time March arrives there is a faint stirring of expectation as I remember that winter doesn't last forever, it only seems to. The birds that tough it out with me help keep alive my fragile optimism and remind me that there have been better days and that more will come.

Just as winter birds brighten that dreary season, so there are compensations in old age. Many joys we once knew have departed just as the warblers leave and the wood thrush grows silent at summer's end. Melodies of our earlier years are muted and we miss the bright exhilarations like the robins and the bluebirds. But we are not left without other hardier joys that make up in endurance for what they may lack in color. Just as there are songs in the night of suffering there are delights of the last miles of the way.

Best of all, there is the glorious assurance that we are

headed for eternal springtime. Heaven knows no aging, no winters. That blessed prospect is the brightest angel of old age. There are other companions, precious memories, accumulated wisdom, and sturdier faith born of experience. There are some joys that youth and middle age simply cannot know. Some fruits ripen in a later season. Some birds that we had all summer mean more in winter, and there are some treasures in life that increase in value by reason of age. They outlast other things and abide when so much has departed.

I am thankful for the birds of winter. I am grateful for the delights of declining years.

46

Along About Milking Time

This afternoon I strolled across the street from where I live into a little patch of woods on the University campus. I stopped awhile to listen to a wood thrush sing just like his forbears sang when I was a boy. On the little farm where I grew up we kept a cow and mother milked the cow (do I hear groans from Women's Lib?) each late afternoon. The wood thrush was always at his best at that time and mother called him *the milking-time bird.* How sweet his vespers as I, a hungry little country boy, waited for my supper of cornbread and milk!

A lot of water has run under the bridge since then. This young generation never heard of milking time; they know only about milk in cartons. Today I ride in jets and I have watched men walk on the moon. Science has devised wonders beyond description, and if I could tell my father about them, he would write me off as a lunatic. But such is the course of history and such is the path of progress that what promised to bring us to Paradise has landed us in pandemonium and we have been hoisted on our own petard.

A few moments in the woods while I listen to a wood thrush sing bring back precious memories with balm for a fevered spirit and medicine for the soul. It helps to hear something that has not changed with the years nor been updated to keep step with what somebody misnamed Progress. A lot of sophisticates, using up reams of good paper to write nothing, would do well to find a spot somewhere, if find it one can, sufficiently removed from roaring planes, screeching automobiles, and demonic music from hell belched from TV and transistor.

I cannot turn time backward sixty years in its flight for the time machine has no reverse gear, but recollection transcends time and place.

> Precious memories, unseen angels,
> Sent from somewhere to my soul,
> How they linger ever near me,
> And the sacred past unfold.
> Precious memories, how they linger!
> How they ever flood my soul!
> In the stillness of the midnight,
> Precious sacred scenes unfold.
> J. B. F. WRIGHT

What we need is not more sophistication and expertise. We need to get away and hear a wood thrush sing his vespers—along about milking time.

47

The "Withness" of It

The New Testament is full of it. "Dead *with* Christ" (*see* Romans 6:8; Colossians 2:20)—that is our blessed position. When He died, we died, and we are to count it as a present fact. We have been "crucified *with* Him" (*see* Galatians 2:20). But we are also "risen with Him" (*see* Colossians 3:1) to walk in newness of life. We are both dead and alive *with* Him and our state should match our standing. We have been "quickened together *with* Christ" (*see* Ephesians 2:5). Our life is "hid *with* Christ in God" (*see* Colossians 3:3). This is not merely a lot of theological gobbledygook which we are supposed to make ourselves enjoy without knowing what it means. It was all accomplished for us federally when He died and rose from the grave. It tells us what we are and where we are *with* Christ. A string of zeros means nothing but with a numeral at the head it becomes millions. We have no value in ourselves but *with* Him we take on a wealth and importance immeasurable. We are married to Christ if we are Christians and we bear a new name, CHRISTians.

But we are not only *with* Him in position but also in practice. He Himself said: "He that is not with me is against me [that is our position]; and he that gathereth not with me scattereth abroad [that is our practice]" (Matthew 12:30). He is the Great Gatherer and we gather with Him as fishers of men, winning others to this glorious *witness*, this relationship and fellowship, both dead and alive *with* Him.

And the best is still ahead. Somebody said, "The pay in God's service may seem small but the retirement benefits are *out of this world!*" Our Lord prayed that His disciples might be *with* Him where He is. (*See* John 17:24.) We stand in awe of the world to come but Jesus made heaven a *homey* place. He told us that in His Father's House are many mansions and that He was going to prepare a place for us. If it were not so, He said, He would have told us. We have His word for it. It is God's heaven and all God's family will feel at home. Mind you, our Lord went back to heaven in a body. He did not use His Resurrection body merely as a temporary arrangement in order to make Himself known. It was not a spirit, for spirits do not have flesh and bones, He pointed out. In His new body He talked, ate food, was touchable. He is somebody and heaven is a place. All the dead saints are *with* Him and all saints will be given new bodies at the resurrection. We shall be caught up together *with* the saints now departed and so will we ever be *with* the Lord. What the Christian dead are like just now is not explained in detail but they are spirits *with* the Lord. They are not apparitions nor ghosts. Maclaren says, "If a spirit can be localized in a body, I suppose it can be localized without a body." It must have some form of manifestation. It has not been revealed—we do not perfectly comprehend—in just what form Moses and Elijah came back at the Transfiguration. Our present faculties could not take it in if it were explained.

Let it be enough to say:

> *With* Christ! No more is told.
> What more, Lord, couldst Thou tell?
> This is enough to satisfy
> The heart that loves Thee well.
>
> ALEXANDER MACLAREN

We do know that to be *with* Christ is far, far better. We will let it go at that for now. And thank God for the *with*ness!

48

Look Who's Here!

Jesus was in the house of Jairus in answer to a hurried call to heal a sick daughter. On the way over He had been detained for a few moments when a very sick woman pressed through the crowd to touch the hem of His garment. It reminds us of how, when a similar urgent

call came from Mary and Martha at Bethany, our Lord
did not hurry but abided two more days where He was.
He let both the sick daughter and Lazarus die and then
arrived to raise them from the dead. He could afford to
take His time!

Before He arrived someone from the house of Jairus
met the ruler and said, ". . . Thy daughter is dead: why
troublest thou the Master any further?" (Mark 5:35). It
was too late by ordinary reckoning but it is never too late
when Jesus is on His way! In the house He said to the
mourners, "Weep not; she is not dead but sleepeth."
(*See* verse 39.) He had said that about Lazarus. To Him
death was and is but a sleep and that does not mean
spiritual unconsciousness. Even in natural sleep we
dream.

Luke tells us that when Jesus said this, they laughed
Him to scorn, *knowing that she was dead*. To them she
was dead and that was the end of everything. That is as
far as atheism, agnosticism, infidelity, and unbelief
ever get. Everything is just cause and effect—cold
natural law—and when you're dead you're dead. The
scoffers of the last days, Peter tells us, laugh at the prospect of Christ's return and they use the same old argument, ". . . all things continue as they were from the
beginning of the creation" (2 Peter 3:4). But Jesus Christ
is Lord of all and He operates on both sides of death,
here and hereafter. "Knowing that she was dead" is not
the end of the matter.

Bearers of sad news, as in this account, often tell the
Christian who has called on Jesus in the hour of desperation, "It's no use. Why bother the Lord?" Death is never
the last word for a Christian for there is always the resur-

rection. And in many another emergency when the situation looks hopeless the scoffers again and again have laughed too soon. When Jesus Christ is in the room, all the conclusions of mortal men fall short. At Jacob's well the Samaritan woman said, "Thou hast nothing to draw with and the well is deep." (*See* John 4:11.) That was correct but it did not cover the issue. The disciples on the way to Emmaus lamented that it was now the third day since the crucifixion. That was correct but Jesus was walking with them when they said it! Martha affirmed her belief that Lazarus would rise in the resurrection but before her stood the Resurrection and the Life! When Jesus ordered that the stone be rolled away from the sepulcher, this same Martha objected that it would not be advisable since Lazarus had been dead four days! One is tempted to cry, "So what!" When Jesus Christ is on the scene all other calculations must be revaluated. Even in the presence of death He makes a difference!

"Knowing that she was dead." "The well is deep." "It has been three days since Calvary." "Lazarus has been dead four days." *So what!* What difference does all that and everything else make if Jesus Christ is here!

He promised to attend every meeting where even two or three gather in His name. I wonder what would happen if some droll Wednesday night prayer meeting ever took Him seriously! It might not break up before morning if we could forget all the "yes, buts." Most of our meetings add up to, "We know you're here, Lord . . . BUT . . . ."

It's about time we met all these wise objections, reservations, and qualifications with one big hearty *So what! Look who's here!*

49

The Underprivileged

I do not mean what you think. We do have the less fortunates, the millions without advantages, the hungry millions without a decent chance for living, education, promotion, or success. I mean the modern, affluent, young generation with every conceivable provision for good living, but who do not know what good living is, who are surfeited with what money can buy but are bankrupt in what it cannot buy.

I grew up in the hills at the beginning of this century. My early days would be viewed with pity today, but life had a simplicity, a flavor, a taste unknown to modern mortals. They are the truly underprivileged, but they would give you a blank stare if you suggested it.

If you did not grow up in the hills down South; if you never woke up to the song of the mockingbird; if you never picked cotton, went possum hunting, attended corn-shuckings and country singings; if you never trudged to a country schoolhouse with a piece of fatback and a sweet potato for lunch—if you missed all this— then your privileges are forever gone. I do not pity my schoolmates of those days. I pity you. I know it is wasted pity and I cannot tell you what you really missed for you have no way of comprehending it. No automobile to drive to school! no atom bombs, no jets, no television, no trips to the moon—just living. There was more real pleasure in walking through a frosty meadow to see whether your rabbit trap had snared a bunny than in all the phony ecstasies of the delirium tremens called progress.

All who have missed the pattern of living, when times were gentler, deserve our pity. They can never recover it and they cannot imagine what it was like. It is portrayed in books and movies that truly cannot convey any adequate sense of the original. There is a nostalgia for it among the rat-racers today with all their stimulants and tranquilizers, their jogging along home from the health food stores. But time will not turn backward in its flight and this is the point of no return. You can't go home again and yesterday will not become today.

Of necessity I have to belong to the privileged class today. I've been modernized. I wrote some of this aboard a jet! But I did know the other and its memory stands me in good stead as I make my way through the pandemonium we had mistaken in the distance for Paradise. I really claim proudly membership in the underprivileged class of another day.

The old faith is smiled upon indulgently or smiled upon as *corny* by the sophisticates of today. They do not know that we oldtimers also smilingly tolerate them! Like Paul and Silas in the Philippian jail we would say, ". . . Do thyself no harm: for we are all here!" (Acts 16:28). As to what is privilege, it all depends. We'd be glad to swap a lot of the advantages of this age for some of the privileges of yesteryears. But we can't get together—talk about a communications gap, this is it!

Anyway, let's get it straight as to who the so-called underprivileged really are!

50

Waiting

Always she waited.

For years she waited for someone. She knew not who it was until we met and then she knew and so did I! After that, until we married, she waited for me to come in from preaching trips and, no matter where I had been, the return trip was always by her home.

I was a half-sick preacher with not much money starting out in an uncertain, new traveling ministry. In 1940 she joined me and in those days of rail travel we waited together for trains at all hours. Every kind of depot all over the country saw us surrounded by baggage, just waiting. I always wanted to go early and was in the Greensboro depot before the coming train had ever left Danville, Virginia!

When I traveled alone and she was at home, she waited for my daily telephone call or my letter. Sometimes the mail was late and that day was not complete.

We sent Special Deliveries for Sunday to bridge the weekend gap.

The day came when the planes took over. She did not like to fly but she flew and for more precious years we waited in airports and little dreamed how short our time together remained to enjoy.

She was stricken by a strange weird malady and for six months fought a losing fight. Her last note in the hospital was hardly legible, handed to me when I left for a few hours' rest. It read, "When are you coming back?" She is still waiting for me to come. Nothing can shake my assurance that I shall make it and find her waiting with Christ which is far, far, better. What her spirit is like, how she manifests herself, I do not know. She is asleep in Jesus but alive and aware. Nothing can make me believe that a love life so precious all those years will be crushed and thrown away. God will not grow a flower that exquisite just to throw it to the ground.

> Can the bonds that make us here
> Know ourselves immortal,
> Drop away like foliage rare
> At life's inner portal?
> What is holiest here below
> Must forever live and grow.

And I believe that she waits for *me*, call it wishful thinking if you will. I agree with Dr. John A. Broadus. With Matthew 22:30 in mind, he says, "There is nothing here to forbid the persuasion that the relations of earthly life will be remembered in the future state, the persons recognized, and special affections cherished with delight."

Whatever is in the will of God here will come to full fruition. He who began a good work here will perfect it. To be sure, we do not marry over there but any bonds so precious as to be a figure of our union with Christ and His church will be glorified. Nothing is lost and what is good here will be better there. I believe my dear one waits for *me*. The hymn books are full of that longing for fulfillment. God will honor the faith that says,

Somehow, somewhere, meet we must . . .

.   .   .   .

Life is ever lord of death
And love can never lose its own.
JOHN GREENLEAF WHITTIER

God would not be a Father if He denied in the next world that which, next to salvation, brought deepest joy to our hearts down here.

Eternal be the sleep
If not to waken so!
JOHN LOCKHART

51

"No Night There"

Summer is passing and the days grow shorter, the nights longer. I feel like taking off for Australia where the season is turning toward spring. I am never happier than when the days begin to lengthen. I am an early riser and summer is made to order for me. Long ago I suffered for several years from nervous exhaustion. I was plagued with insomnia and dreaded to see the coming of night. Now I sleep like a child; however, I suppose there is something left over from those troubled years. I know that night is the Lord's arrangement for our rest, although millions of Americans spend most of their evenings doing everything but resting. Look out on any great city in the middle of the night and you wonder when people sleep!

Job evidently did not relish the hours of darkness: "When I lie down, I say, When shall I arise, and the night be gone? and I am full of tossings to and fro unto the dawning of the day" (Job 7:4). Paul thought of this age as a night far spent with day at hand (Romans 13:12). He wrote, ". . . we are not of the night, nor of darkness" (1 Thessalonians 5:5). The Scriptures abound in references to night as a time of sorrow, of loneliness, of trouble, and always with a longing like the passengers on Paul's voyage to Rome who cast four anchors and wished for the day (Acts 27:29).

Most precious of all is John's word from Patmos concerning the Heavenly City: "There shall be no night there" (Revelation 21:25; 22:5). Down here "the night cometh when no man can work." So much to do and so little time! But heaven speaks of continual and eternal fulfillment with no broken dreams, no unfinished tasks. Heaven is not an everlasting vacation. ". . . his servants shall serve him" (Revelation 22:3). I have never been a loafer here and I am not interested in sitting on a cloud strumming a harp forever. Freed from our present limitations and with an eternity in which to do it, we shall serve and praise the Lord. It will always be daylight—not our kind of daylight but the eternal light of God's presence. Since we never grow weary, we shall need no rest. Yet we shall rest as we work without the frictions and irritations of these frustrating days. I have read that the gates of that city are never shut since there is no night and no need of protection where no one shall hurt or destroy. Darkness is associated with evil and Satan is its prince. The forces under him are called the powers of darkness. In the age to come he is definitely out of business, put away in a lake of fire far removed from the City of Light.

God has allowed us compensations for darkness in this present life—sleep, the stars, songs in the night. Some of life's greatest experiences have come to the children of God under cover of darkness. We must make the most of it, and there is a great deal to be made of it! Hereafter we shall have no need of the lessons we learn here, for we shall see everything under better light no longer blinded by our eyes.

"The night is far spent, the day is at hand . . ." (Romans 13:12). The psalmist wrote: "My soul waiteth for the Lord more than they that watch for the morning . . ." (Psalms 130:6). Night belongs to the old order which will end when my Lord takes over. We are children of the Day. There is no place for darkness in that Day. Evil men welcome the night when they can carry out their dark designs. It is obvious that such men would be out of place in heaven. It is also obvious that we who are headed for eternal day should walk as children of the day before we arrive.

52

Almost Time to Go

I am preaching this week in Buffalo, New York. My room looks out on a little lake surrounded by trees in all their autumn glory. Wild ducks paddle along the placid waters. They should be leaving soon for the south. And so should I! I am not returning home for it takes at least two to make a home and now there is only an apartment. But it is south and the farther south the better I like it.

How wonderful the instinct that God has planted in the breast of every wildfowl to know when it is time to go! The poet said rightly that He who guides the homing bird will lead our steps aright. It is almost time to start toward another clime after a long stay in this old world. I perceive an inner instinct that longs for the land that is fairer than day. I have enjoyed it here and the old earth is still beautiful though fouled up by the Evil One. I expect to come back and walk around when it has been taken over by my Lord and set in order. But for now and until then I can only say, "To depart and be with Christ is far better."

This picture card view from my window these crisp autumn days means so much to a tired pilgrim. The children of God are citizens of another country and they grow homesick for heaven. Alas, some of them settle down in the barnyards of this world and feed too much on what they find there. They grow fat and foul and lose their impulse to rise and join their fellow-migrants to a better land. Abraham looked for a city with foundations. The only foundations he knew down here were tent pegs driven in desert sands. Paul languished in prison and said, ". . . the time of my departure is at hand" (2 Timothy 4:6).

I feel like saying to the ducks on the lake outside my window, "Have a good trip. You will know when it is time to start." And I must make ready for a better country. It is almost time to go.

I do not find much of this spirit among church folk today. You would never suspect that we are pilgrims and strangers, exiles and aliens, just passing through. The talk is mostly of eating and drinking, marrying and giving in marriage, buying and selling, planting and building. I see ornate churches, I ride in plush cars and visit

posh parsonages. We are living well. The new
philosophy seems to be that God would have every
Christian be a millionaire. I know that holiness is not
synonymous with hair shirts, but I am not yet accus-
tomed to the new variety of clergyman in gambler's garb
looking more like he was headed for Las Vegas than for
church. When have I heard "In the Sweet By and By"?

If the saints don't watch out, the Big Freeze is going to
overtake us paddling around here. It has already reached
most of our parishes. The new affluence is not conducive
to pilgrim living. TV all day long and half the night does
not help. The rat race for a bigger house, one more car,
country-clubbing and the new life-styles make poor
background for a spiritual revival.

The old concept of a weary traveler passing up Vanity
Fair for Heaven is out these days, but it is still in the
Book, my official guide for the trip. So I still feel an
old-fashioned urge to say to the ducks, "I'm all primed
for departure. It's almost time to go."

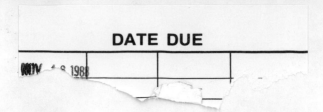

DATE DUE

NOV 1 8 1988		